SIDECHICKS

MARRIED TO THE VISIONARY

PATRICE MEADOWS

SIDECHICKS

MARRIED TO THE VISIONARY

PATRICE MEADOWS

Copyright Notice

SIDECHICKS
MARRIED TO THE VISIONARY
Patrice Meadows

© 2018, Patrice Meadows
www.patricemeadows.com
info@patricemeadows.com

Published by Anointed Fire
www.anointedfire.com
Cover Design by Justin Hardin
Author photograph by Alwon Mayweather

ISBN-13: 978-1985864306
ISBN-10: 1985864304

Disclaimer

Dedication

⇢ This book is dedicated to my husband, Bryan Meadows. I want to thank him for marrying me. I'm just a little girl from Maryland trying to find her way. I'm rough around the edges, and I consistently resist your pressing, but I'm nonetheless grateful that you found me. Without your vision and consistency in pursuing the will of God for our lives, I wouldn't be a Sidechick married to a visionary. Your vision inspires me, challenges me and gives me a reason to keep fighting. Thank you for making me better, wiser, stronger and more loving. I am forever grateful to you.

⇢ And to my rambunctious daughter. You are the best gift God could have ever given me. You are my true miracle child. Before you were born, I had a heart that had been broken many times over, but you have shown me unconditional love and a reason to believe again. I love you with all my heart and am truly blessed to have you as my child. Thank you for being so loving and helpful. The world is truly not ready for you!

Acknowledgments

→I want to acknowledge all those who have prayed me through the writing process. I had this book in my heart for many years but lacked the confidence and strategy to get it done.

→I want to thank Tiffany Buckner and the Remnant Writers for giving me the tools I needed to become an author. Your instruction and understanding have taught me invaluable skills in my pursuit to share my experience with the world through writing.

→I also want to thank Justin Hardin for providing the graphics for this book. Your creative design allowed me to see this book completed and to work harder to make sure it was finished.

→I also want to thank my Embassy family for holding me accountable. Not a week went by that someone didn't ask me when my book was coming out. My dedication to serving you all has pushed me to complete this work.

→Last, but certainly not least, I want to honor my mom and dad. It is your consistent hard work and insistence that your children succeed that have allowed me to be where I am today. I watched you work tirelessly to provide for our family. When life dealt you a blow, you never lost your fight. I honor you for providing my education and showing me persistence so that I can serve the world. God bless you!

Table of Contents

Introduction

An old adage says, "Behind every great man is a great woman." However, this statement falls short of the truth. Great women don't stand behind great men; they stand beside them. I boldly venture to say that they sometimes have to stand in front (more on this to come). In God's original plan for humanity, man and woman together received the blessing to fill the Earth and have dominion. Women are not second-class citizens or less important than men. In fact, women have a significant role in families and societies.

Challenging the inferiority mindset and every misled idea of what a woman should be is the sole purpose of this book. Specifically, using biblical and modern examples of women married to great men will form the basis on which we build our case. Women married to great men possess a few key characteristics. Identifying these characteristics will help establish an understanding of the role, function and importance of women in families and society. Whether you are single or married, it is critical that you identify and grow these characteristics in your life.

For a single woman, understanding the significant role you play will help you identify the wrong man when he surely comes. If he doesn't pull on the characteristics of the Sidechick who lies within you, he may not be the one or he may not be the one for you right now. I believe many women have found themselves dating and married to the wrong men because they failed to understand who they were and what they were called to do as women. When you have a revelation of your purpose, you will recognize a man who connects with and aligns with the vision you have for your life. Although this is not necessarily a relationship book, it will impact the current and future relationships that you establish. You will no longer see your relationships as simple love stories, but you will see your relationships as tools for the manifestation of God's perfect plan. You will no longer enter into covenant haphazardly, but you will instead take careful thought of the commitments you make. You will value your contributions to a relationship and never allow someone to undermine your worth again. My prayer is that you will avoid the mistakes that we as a woman often make in choosing a mate. Beyond having better relationships, you will find greater joy in who you are as a woman of God.

For the married woman, this book will help affirm your decision to remain married. You will understand your responsibility to God, your husband, and your family. My prayer is that you also find a renewed sense of passion, purpose, and the pursuit of the calling of God on your life as a woman and as a wife. Whatever you have been through, whatever challenges you currently face, you will know that you can overcome them and have a marriage after God's own heart. May you connect with a woman featured in this book and see yourself in her story.

For the woman who is divorced, this book is for you as well. May you find hope in this book, understand what went wrong, and find the motivation and strength to move forward. Understand that God's grace is sufficient for you too. God is very much concerned with your relationship status and you redefining your image of yourself. May you never feel guilt or shame for your story but instead, find encouragement. You may have made a mistake, or your marriage may not have gone as planned, but the blood of the Lamb already redeems you.

This book is for every woman. Regardless of your age or marital status, there are characteristics that every woman should possess to some degree. Depending on the specific call of God on your life, you may find that you possess and utilize some qualities more often than others. If you are currently single, you will prepare for your role as a wife or find a greater level of understanding of your responsibility to your local assembly and your family. I want to convince every single woman not to wait around for her husband to find her. Instead, work to build the qualities you need to be a good wife while you wait. Find yourself, serve God and serve the body of Christ. Your husband will find you when you have surrendered to the purpose and plan of God for your life. Commitment could be detrimental to your future.

Due to my personal experience and the experiences of the women whose stories are told here, we will focus on women married to "great" men. Pastors, politicians, apostles, actors, prophets, entrepreneurs, professional athletes and doctors to name a few. These may be the common titles society leads us to believe are "great" men. However, I hope that you will discover the great king and priest in the man that you are currently married to or will eventually marry in the future. It is important that we have a revelation of who our man is so that we never devalue or disrespect him.

The same theory applies to single women working to fulfill the vision of a local assembly of believers. Throughout this book, I will correlate the church to a marriage. Single women should serve God through their local churches. This is the best preparation for the service you will render in marriage. The pastor, as the head of the church, can be juxtaposed to the role of a husband in a marriage. Leading is part of the man's function. He is the visionary of the house. Every woman should attend a church with a vision. Likewise, every woman should marry a man with a vision. Otherwise, you will find yourself frustrated trying to follow a man who is not leading you anywhere.

When you are married to a visionary, you will undeniably find yourself also married to the vision. Whether the vision is starting a school, building a church, launching a music career or achieving world peace, saying "I do" to a visionary means you take on the responsibility of seeing that vision come to pass. Your time, your family, your gifts, your financial resources and even your body all become tools for propelling the vision from a dream to reality. I remember a couple of years after getting married when there were constantly people in our home. We had Bible study and worship services weekly, often inviting strangers into our personal space. On one instance, people were coming in off the street who'd heard music and prayer and wanted to join. We hosted guests from all over the country and opened our home to people who didn't have a place to stay. We did this for several years. Many years later, written on the walls and marked on the floors of our home are the stories of the sacrifices we made. Forever ingrained in the landscape of our home is a reminder of the vision we committed our lives to fulfill.

Whether you marry into the vision or are part of its inception, the task can be daunting at times. But there is good news! You don't have to do it alone. God has given you the tools you need to support the vision and to help bring it to pass. Ingrained in every fiber of your being are the qualities, gifts and abilities you need to stand beside your visionary and work the vision to fruition.

The term Sidechick has been made popular by mainstream media and is often used to describe a woman who is involved in an extramarital affair. I would like to identify the origin and re-establish the dignity and meaning of the term Sidechick. If you are offended by the term Sidechick, you may not be ready for the revelation this book brings. As a "help meet", what exactly have you been called to do? What is your purpose? How do you fit into the plan of fulfilling the vision of God? This book is here to help you discover your God-given purpose as a woman married to the visionary, and as a result, also married to the vision. You will follow the lives of many women throughout the Bible and history. While reading their stories, you will identify the characteristics of every successful *Sidechick* and determine how to grow that quality in your life. Join this journey of self-realization, empowerment and revelation. You are critical to the fulfillment of the vision and well-equipped to do so. May you find comfort in knowing you are a *Sidechick*, designed and built by God for such a time as this.

CHAPTER 1

Help Meet

Arranged marriage, as was the custom in her culture, she would soon meet the man her father picked out for her to marry. The man would then decide whether to proceed with the marriage or call it off and keep looking. Nervous was an understatement. She'd prepared her entire life to be ready for this day.

"What if he doesn't like me?" she asked. "He would be crazy not to," replied her mother. "You're beautiful, humble, hardworking and smart. Any man would love to have you as his wife."

She spent the rest of the day praying and pampering. In less than an hour, she would face her future mate. She couldn't help but think if she had done enough to prepare. Was *she ready to leave home and be a wife? Were her hair, skin and nails beautiful enough? All of these questions and more raced through her mind as the set time approached. And then, he arrived. Along with her mother, father, brother and two sisters, she went outside to meet him. They stood in a line in front of their home as his car approached. He arrived with his mother and father. The car stopped, he stepped out and scanned the line her family had formed. Then, he walked right up to her, took her hands in his and said, "My wife."*

To believe that men and women were created equal does not make me a feminist, it makes me a Biblicist. Society would like us to believe that it is abnormal to think that men and women were created equal. With unequal pay, a barrage of sexual harassment cases, women lacking the right to vote, denial to formal education and other evidence from around the world, one might believe that women are inferior to men. But this is NOT God's intention. Genesis chapter 1 explains:

*And God said, Let us make man in our image, after our likeness: and let **them** have dominion over the fish of the sea, and over the fowl of the air, and over the cattle, and over all the earth, and over every creeping thing that creepeth upon the earth. o God created man in his image, in the image of God created he him; **male and female** created him **them**. And God blessed **them,** and God said unto **them**, Be fruitful, and multiply, and replenish the earth, and subdue it: and have dominion over the fish of the sea, and over the fowl of the air, and over every living thing that moveth upon the earth.*

Note that the blessing God released was over man *and* woman. "And God blessed *them."* The woman was not an afterthought. She was already inside of Adam when he was made. God had a particular plan from the beginning to bring the woman out of the man at the appointed time. Man and woman were created as one from the beginning. Later, God

3

differentiated a woman from a man by forming her from Adam's rib. Even after God had created man and all the animals, there was still something missing. If Adam was to fulfill the blessing released over him, he needed Eve.

The blessing God commanded for Adam and Eve was twofold. They were to:

1. Be fruitful
2. Have dominion

Being Fruitful

To be fruitful means to be productive or to reproduce. When you are productive, you put work or effort in, and you get a result out. The type of result depends on the work you put in. For example, someone is productive in the gym if that person gains strength or loses weight. Someone is productive in a business if he or she is profitable. It is also helpful to understand what it looks like when you are unproductive. Someone is unproductive if that person spends years in a romantic relationship and don't get married. An employee is unproductive if he or she works at the same company, in the same position for ten years and never receives a promotion. God designed us to be productive. We go from glory to glory and from faith to faith. Our work was designed to be fruitful.

God not only blessed Adam and Eve to be fruitful, but God also blessed the animals and told them to be fruitful too. In Genesis 2:22, the author writes:

> *And God blessed them (the animals), saying, Be fruitful, and multiply, and fill the waters in the seas, and let fowl multiply in the earth.*

In the beginning, God created a finite amount of beings, possibly several hundred thousand different species, but still a fixed amount. He rested on the sixth day, looked at His creation and saw that it was good. He had placed everything inside the Earth that was needed to sustain humankind for the rest of eternity. In His infinite wisdom, He created a system of endless supply through a process called reproduction.

Produce and reproduce. This is what God has called men and women to do in the Earth. We are to grow everything He has given us, including our families, our faith, our financial resources and other followers of Jesus Christ.

John 15: 5-8 put it this way:

> *I am the vine; ye are the branches: He that abideth in me, and I in him, the same bringeth forth much fruit: for without me ye can do nothing. Herein is my Father glorified, that ye bear much fruit; so shall ye be my disciples.*

In other words, the evidence of a true follower of Jesus Christ is someone who produces fruit. Adam simply could not be fruitful without Eve. He could till the ground

6

and cause vegetation to replenish the Earth, but to reproduce himself, he had to come together with Eve.

At this point, God had not differentiated man from animal. The responsibility of both man and animal was to make more of themselves and replenish the Earth. The differentiation comes when God commands man to have dominion.

Have dominion

Dominion means sovereignty or control. God left a man in charge of the earth realm. Man and woman together had power over every other living being. If anything was to happen on the Earth, the man had to allow it or cause it to be.

For a man to live out the blessing that God commanded, he needed the woman. The story, according to Genesis 2:20-23 tells us:

> *But for Adam, there was not found a help meet for him. And the Lord God caused a*

deep sleep to fall upon Adam, and he slept: and he took one of his ribs, and closed up the flesh instead thereof; And the rib, which the Lord God had taken from man, made he a woman, and brought her unto the man. And Adam said, this is now bone of my bones, and flesh of my flesh: she shall be called Woman because she was taken out of Man.

This selection of scriptures is rich with revelation and meaning. However, I will focus on two key points from this passage related to the role of Sidechicks:

1. It was not good for man to be alone.
2. Adam was sleep, but woke up and knew Eve.

It was not good for man to be alone

This passage from Genesis tells us that God created Eve to be a help meet for Adam. While many translations make this sound like an assistant position, I want to challenge this thought. Biblical scholars explain that the word help meet comes from the Hebrew words *ezer* and *k'enegdo*. When you understand the meanings of each of these words, you gain revelation of God's intention for a woman. The Hebrew word *ezer* is found in the Bible 21 times. It means to surround or protect. It can also be translated to mean savior. This word is most often used in the Bible referring to what God is to man. For example, in Psalm 33:20, David says, "*Our soul waiteth for the Lord, he is our help and our shield.*" The word help is translated as *ezer*.

I believe God was telling Adam that Eve was coming to save or deliver him. Deliver him from what, you might ask. Her job was to deliver him from loneliness or possibly to be unable to fulfill the blessing of God alone. Women have the ability and responsibility to "save men." Unfortunately, many women fall into the trap of becoming a man's mother. This is a terrible, albeit common mistake. The role of a mother is that of a nurturer and a superior. Instead, the role of a wife is equal, although different role. There are some responsibilities that a wife takes on that the mother once had like cooking and cleaning. However, a real man does not want his wife controlling his life. He wants an equal with which he can share ideas and engage in intellectual conversations with. He wants someone who can encourage him, all the while, meeting his physical needs. The word *ezer* is mentioned over 12 times in the Old Testament, signifying its importance. Two of these references were to women, while the other ten referred to God.

The Hebrew word *k'enegdo* is only mentioned one time in scripture. What a wonderful compliment it is that God reserved something special to explain woman in His word! Nevertheless, this also makes it difficult to ascertain an exact meaning of this word. The word *k'enegdo* means against, in front of or the opposite. These terms appear to have different meanings until you take a deeper look at the definitions in unison. One scholar, Diana Webb[1], explains that "this word would mean like looking into a mirror." Women are the opposite of men and, in turn, hold the qualities missing in men. We form a complete picture of everything needed to fulfill God's calling. Another Jewish scholar says that the word *k'enegdo* means corresponding to or equal in power.

Ephesians 5:21-25 says:

> *Submitting yourselves one to another in fear of God. Wives, submit yourselves unto your husbands, as unto the Lord. For the husband is the head of the wife, even as Christ is the head of the church: and he is the saviour of the body. Therefore as the church is subject unto Christ, so let the wives be to their husbands in everything.*

[1]

http://www.womeninthescriptures.com/2010/11/real-meaning-of-term-help-meet.html

Husbands, love your wives, even as Christ also loved the church, and gave himself for it.

I want to clarify that, although men and women were created spiritually equal, they have different roles. Many marriages get stuck in a fight over roles. Eventually, it becomes a fight about love and respect or submission and equality. Often, strong women know they are equal, but fail to acknowledge or give space for the man's role in the marriage. Just because you can do something does not mean you should do it.

Ephesians 5:28-29 says:

So ought men to love their wives as their bodies. He that loveth his wife loveth himself. For no man ever yet hated his flesh; but nourisheth and cherisheth it, even as the Lord the church.

Men are to love their wives as themselves. This is because a woman is part of the man's body. The role of man as the head of the home allows for there to be order and a clear process of fulfilling God's plan. Without this order, marriages would constantly hit a wall when decisions need to be made and disputes need to be settled. Somewhere in history, men took this to mean women were to be treated as property, pushed around and not given any freedom. However, the Bible is clear when it explains that men are to love their wives and women are to submit to their husbands in the same manner as between Christ and the church.

Modern society would have us believe that it is okay and even ideal to stay single … to be independent and do your own thing and to despise marriage and the structure, humility and selflessness that it requires. But the Bible is clear on God's original design and plan for mankind. Man and woman together were to replenish the Earth, subdue it and have dominion over every living thing. If you are single, your status does not make you substandard. There is plenty vision for you to be married to, including the work of the Lord and the vision of your local church until your time for marriage comes.

Adam was asleep but woke up and knew Eve

Adam was asleep when God pulled Eve from his rib. This leads to another revelation that Genesis1:28 establishes. Adam awoke from his sleep and recognized Eve. It is critical that a man understands who he is and what he is called by God to do before getting married. How can a man recognize who a woman is in his life if the man doesn't even know who he is? Granted, a man will uncover aspects of his assignment as he gets older and closer to God. However, he should have some idea of where he is going. My husband uses this analogy all the time: Would you get into a car and start driving, not knowing where you are going? In the same manner, you should not enter into covenant with someone not knowing where you intend to go. If you do, you will likewise run out of gas (energy or enthusiasm) before reaching your destination.

Knowing who he is will undoubtedly help a man to identify his wife when he meets her. He will recognize the woman designed to help him fulfill the call on his life. This is also critical in helping the man to recognize his future wife's significance in his life. He will not mistreat this woman when he knows her value. When women understand this assignment, they won't be so infatuated with the outward appearance, a man's bank account or other fleeting characteristics. Marriage also won't be as burdensome when working for a higher calling than it would be if you were just working to make yourself and someone else happy. You will work relentlessly and tirelessly to complete your assignment. Although you will experience some rewards in this lifetime, your true reward will be in Heaven. Remember, you are designed to be a help-meet, a savior, and an equal but opposite force. You are necessary to fulfill the promise and obtain the blessing of God.

CHAPTER 2

Built

For Christmas, I took my daughter to a famous toy store, but this was not your average toy store. Here, the kids are put to work. They choose what kind of stuffed animal they want to make. They pick out the outer shell and then stuff it with filling. They decide if they want to add a beating heart or use different colored string to close the toy. Once the toy is stuffed, they go to the clothing store. Here, they can dress their creation with almost anything they would like. Dresses, jewelry, shoes, hats, skates; the list is almost endless. After dressing and picking out accessories, they take their stuffed animal to the naming zone. Here, they enter in information about what they've made. They input the birthdate, eye color, weight and any other identifying information. Finally, they give their creation a name. A birth certificate

*is printed, and then you can take home your
custom stuffed animal. My daughter loved her
new toy. She sleeps with it and tries to take it
on car rides. She calls the toy by name and is
so proud of what she's made.*

*Imagine how much more God is proud of you,
His creation. As you will see in the coming
chapter, God took special care in building you.*

The first time we are introduced to
God's plan for humanity in Genesis 1:26,
which says:

> *Then God said, "Let us make humanity
> in our image, in our likeness, so that
> they may rule over the fish in the sea
> and the birds in the sky, over the
> livestock and all the wild animals, and
> over all the creatures that move along
> the ground.*

The King James version is full of
references to God making and creating
things. In this scripture, the Hebrew word for

make is *âsâh,* which means to accomplish, to appoint or to bring forth. Then, in verse 27, man and woman are first identified by individual names:

> *So God created humankind in his image, in the image of God he created them; male and female he created them.*

The Hebrew word for creating is *bârâ,* which means to choose. So, in this verse, we get an understanding that God brought forth and appointed man and woman together as one. However, He creates them or chooses them for unique purposes.

Women are fashioned

Man and every living creature were made from the dust of the Earth. The Hebrew word for formed is *yâtsâr,* used in Genesis 2:8, which reads:

> *Now the LORD God had planted a garden in the east, in Eden; and there he put the man he had formed.*

Yâtsâr means to mold or squeeze into shape. This same word is used in Isaiah 45:18.

> *For thus saith the LORD that created the heavens; God himself that formed the earth and made it; he hath established it, he created it not in vain, he formed it to be inhabited: I am the LORD, and there is none else.*

Think of a potter molding a piece of clay into something beautiful. This same principle applies to God forming man and animals from the dust of the Earth. If you have a hard piece of clay, you must first apply water to soften it up. For us, this water is the Holy Spirit. Only then can the clay be formed into whatever you desire. If you try to mold a piece of clay (a person) while it is hard, you will injure yourself, or the clay will break into pieces.

Woman of God, it is essential to understand that before trying to influence a man, you must first soften him up. An old idiom says the fastest way to a man's heart is through his stomach. Why? Because if you connect to something he loves, he will connect with you. A wise woman once told me to always make sure my man is fed before proposing anything or requesting anything from him. Whether through prayer, food, intimacy or kind words, women have the authority and ability to influence men. This must be guarded, cherished and used only for Godly purposes, not selfish gain. Ask Eve, Sarah, Deborah, Jezebel, Esther, the woman with the issue of blood, Mary Magdalene and the list goes on and on.

You were built for this!

The woman, in contrast to the other products of creation, was built.

Genesis 2:22 says:

And the rib, which the LORD God had taken from man, <u>made</u> he a woman and brought her unto the man.

The Hebrew word for made used in this passage is *bânâh,* which means to build. When you build something, you carefully put it together. This is describing how God took the rib from Adam's side to create Eve. In addition to being squeezed into shape, like a man and all of the other creations, the woman was constructed piece by piece. I guess that women, like bones, would break under the kind of pressure meant to mold pieces of tough clay. However, women go through a process of being built over time.

Many pieces must come together for a woman to fully execute her purpose in the Earth. Some behaviors and traits come naturally to a woman, but other things must be learned over time and through experience. That is why the Bible says in Titus 2 that older women must teach the younger women.

The aged women likewise, that they are in behaviour as becometh holiness, not false accusers, not given to much wine, teachers of good things. Also, they may teach the young women to be sober, to love their husbands, to love their children, To be discreet, chaste, keepers at home, good, obedient to their husbands, that the word of God is not blasphemed.

It is often said of women that they are stubborn, stuck in their ways and difficult to sway. When you do something wrong to a woman, she will remember it forever. Men, on the other hand, appear to be tough on the outside but are as easy to sway as a fat kid lusting after cake. Understanding how and why we were created brings an unmatched ability to make a marriage work. The things that you may find yourself arguing over in your marriage or just not seeing eye to eye about may be due to the way you were designed. Always seek to understand each other's point of view. Realize that you need your differences to make a marriage work.

If you want to understand your purpose fully, it is necessary to understand your origin. The rib provides great insight into how and why you were created.

The Rib

To understand the significance of the rib, one must understand both the anatomy and physiology of these set of bones. Ultimately, as seen throughout nature, the structure or makeup of a thing is directly tied to its function or purpose. Flowers have colorful petals to draw insects to them for pollination. Monkeys have long arms and toes, enabling them to swing from and climb trees. Numerous examples exist in nature supporting this point. Let's take a closer look at the make-up of a rib to understand its purpose.

Anatomy

Humans have a total of 24 ribs in 12 sets of two. Seven sets of ribs are connected to the spinal column in the back and the sternum (the bone in the front of the chest). The other five sets of ribs are only connected to the spine in the back. See figure 1. The first seven sets of ribs are connected to the sternum by costal cartilage.

Bones of the human thorax

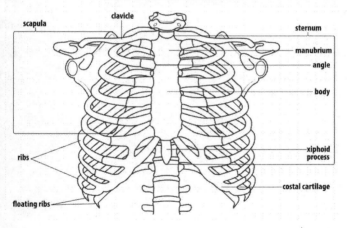

Figure 1. Bones of the human thorax

Cartilage is significant because, unlike bone, it is firm yet flexible. Cartilage is found in high quantities in infants, but is replaced by bone during growth and development. Additionally, cartilage is found in the ear, nose, spinal column and joints between bones. Cartilage is also found at the end of bones where they connect with other bones.

Rib sets 8, 9 and 10 have ends that fuse together. The last two sets of ribs (11 and 12) are known as floating ribs because they only connect to the spinal column in the back and have "floating ends" in the front. The rib cage is made up of costal cartilage and the flat, curved rib bones. All of these attributes of the rib structure are important for the function of the ribs. They also provide an understanding of how and why you were created.

b. Function

The primary job of the ribs is to protect and support.

Protection

The function of the human ribs is to protect the organs of the thorax or chest cavity. The main organs present in the chest cavity are the lungs and the heart. Other important parts of the chest cavity include the spleen, diaphragm, esophagus and several major blood vessels. These blood vessels are responsible for supplying blood from the heart to the brain and the remainder of the body. The blood is important because it carries oxygen and other vital nutrients throughout the body. To damage or block these blood vessels would be fatal to any human being.

In the process of breathing, the lungs expand to let in more oxygen. The flexibility of the cartilage and the structure of the ribs allow the lungs to expand safely. The flat and curved shape of the ribs also protects important blood vessels. If ribs are damaged, they severely inhibit the expansion of the lungs, preventing optimal blood flow.

The ribs not only protect the lungs but also protect the heart. The Bible declares *"Who can discern the heart, for it is deceitfully wicked."* It is a challenging job to protect someone's heart. The person must trust you entirely, and you must always prove yourself to be trustworthy. It is more difficult for a man to recover from an adulterous woman than for a woman to recover from an unfaithful man. The woman was designed to protect a man's heart. So what does he do when the person designed to protect his heart breaks it instead? Some women have discovered this advantage and used it against men. They use their sexuality to manipulate them to get what they want. A woman's job, however, is to protect the heart of the man, taking on the burden of his assignment and working to fulfill the vision God has given him.

Support

The ribs provide insight into the traits of a powerful Sidechick. She must be strong and firm, but also flexible and provide room for her husband to breathe. When a man and woman marry, the man is surely not who he will be in 5, 10 or 20 years. The woman, in the beginning, may need to help provide structure and support. At the beginning of my marriage, I can remember asking myself, "Do I need to explain how to do this or help with that?" Some things occurred naturally to me that my husband didn't seem to know or at least didn't make a priority to complete. For example, making a household budget, preparing and packing for travel or developing a system for laundry. My husband may have had the skill to do all of these things, but it was up to me to provide support for getting these things done. Several years later, he can travel and meet every financial need because of the structure that I took responsibility for setting at the beginning of our marriage.

It is critical for a wife to grow with her husband as he develops spiritually and achieves career and financial success. Don't get stuck in what was or try to continue to provide the same amount of support and structure as at the beginning of the marriage. Grow together, increase together and allow there to be everlasting new life breathed into your marriage. I used to wonder why men would become successful and leave the women behind who helped them achieve that success. Someone may purport that the man became full of himself and wanted to "upgrade." However, my guess is a little more complicated than that hypothesis.

I believe in some instances the woman was stuck at the beginning of the relationship when the money, fame and public pressure didn't exist. As the man became successful, she grew resentful, instead of being supportive. The pain or struggle from the beginning of the marriage is too much for her to accept, even though they have reached a different place. As Sidechicks, like a rib, we must allow there to be room to breathe. Provide support as your husband develops and be a constant source of fresh air, rather than a reminder of the past.

God used a rib to create you and give you purpose. A Sidekick is the ultimate example of the fulfillment of God's promise to Adam. For He said, *"It is not good that man should be alone, I shall make him a help meet."* Like a rib, you are to protect and support the heart (vision) of your husband.

CHAPTER 3

Nameless

For many years, I wondered if she existed. I had heard that she did but never knew for sure. There were no tabloids or true Hollywood stories about her life, but her husband is one of the most famous actors in the world. When you think of every great movie with an African American male star, he is probably in one out of every two. He's on talk shows and radio broadcasts, commercials and ad campaigns around the world. His name is in lights, on billboards and magazine covers. Everyone calls him for interviews, endorsement deals and speaking engagements galore. He walks on red carpets, and accepts Golden Globes, sits in private green rooms and has VIP status wherever he goes.

When you look back at pictures, you see her. But thinking back, you hardly realized she was there. All the reporters focused on her husband, and the fans showered him with love and adoration. The reviews always praised him and left you wanting more. The records show that they've been married for 33 years, but that's all we know of the couple. Unlike most couples in Hollywood, they keep their private life private. He continues to be a trail blazer in the world of Hollywood and leave his mark on entertainment. His name is Denzel Washington, but his wife's name is a name we hardly know.

At the beginning of this book, I challenged an adage that says behind every great man is a great woman. My correction is that great women stand beside great men. This belief forms the basis of the term Sidechick. In many instances, although wives stand beside their great men, they are often overlooked and unrecognized for their contributions to the vision. Even in the Bible, there are stories of men who changed the world, but little mention of their wives. The wife may be sparingly described, not mentioned at all or simply nameless. This chapter is to encourage you and help you to understand that not having a name does not mean you don't have significance.

One great example is that of Noah's nameless wife. Noah's story can be found in Genesis 5-10. He is one of the great patriarchs of our faith. In his time, God was angry because man allowed evil to have its way on Earth. Men were taking multiple wives and producing children with the giants that roamed the Earth. God promised to destroy the men and every living thing on the Earth, but of Noah and his family, the Bible explains in Genesis 6:8:

> *But Noah found grace in the eyes of the LORD. These are the generations of Noah: He was a just man and perfect in his generations, and Noah walked with God.*

Every person and every animal that was on Earth would be destroyed. God hated that He'd created man, seeing what he had become. God would send a flood to destroy everything so that He could start over. But there was one exception in all the Earth, and that was Noah, his family and the male and female of specific animals would be saved. Over the next few chapters, God gave Noah specific instructions. He told Noah of His displeasure with mankind and how He would destroy them with water. Noah was told how to build the ark to save his family and the animals that would reproduce. The specific measurements and requirements were given to Noah and Noah alone. Notice that it is mentioned that Noah had a wife, but she is not given a name in this story. God spoke to Noah and gave him specific instructions. At no point does it say God spoke to his wife.

In Genesis 9:1, after the flood, God gave Noah the same command He'd given Adam after creation.

And God blessed Noah and his sons, and said unto them, be fruitful, and multiply, and replenish the earth.

Again, this blessing was spoken over Noah and his sons. The women were not mentioned. However, just like Adam in the beginning, they needed their wives to fulfill the assignment that God had given them.

As described in Genesis 5:2, the author recounts:

Male and female created he them; and blessed them, and called their name Adam, in the day when they were created.

I am going to juxtapose these two scriptures: Genesis 9:1 and Genesis 1:28. In the very beginning, God blessed THEM. However, after the flood, the Bible only says that God blessed Noah and his sons. Did God only intend to bless men? Had God changed His mind about the role of man and woman?

I don't believe so. But something significant had happened.

In the beginning, man and woman were one. They were both Adam. God released the blessing over them together. Somewhere along the way, Eve stepped out on her own. Notice in Genesis 3 that the serpent spoke to Eve alone. She engaged in conversation with the serpent without her husband's knowledge.

Now, compare that to how God spoke. God spoke to them (Adam and Eve) together as one. He blessed them together. Be very leery of people who try to create a divide between you and your husband. This could be family members who start a conversation with, "Don't tell your husband, but..." or friends who say, "I know your husband wouldn't like this, but..." What may seem like small talk could turn into your greatest downfall. Genesis 3 continues with God suddenly talking to Adam and Eve individually.

*And the Lord God called unto Adam,
and said unto him, Where art thou? And
he said, I heard thy voice in the garden,
and I was afraid because I was naked,
and I hid. And he said, Who told thee
that thou wast naked? Hast thou ate of
the tree, of which I commanded thee
that thou shouldest not eat? And the
man said, The woman whom thou
gavest to be with me, she gave me of the
tree, and I did eat.*

God called to Adam, and Adam spoke
only for himself. He even blamed God for
giving him the woman that put them in their
current predicament. Adam revealed that it
was Eve who gave him to eat of the tree that
he'd commanded them not to eat. So, God
followed the lead of Adam and started
addressing the woman.

*And the Lord God said unto the woman,
What is this that thou hast did? And the
woman said, The serpent beguiled me,
and I did eat. And the Lord God said*

unto the serpent because thou hast done this, thou art cursed above all cattle, and above every beast of the field; upon thy belly shalt thou go, and dust shalt thou eat all the days of thy life. And I will put enmity between thee and the woman, and between thy seed and her seed; it shall bruise thy head, and thou shalt bruise his heel. Unto the woman he said, I will greatly multiply thy sorrow and thy conception; in sorrow, thou shalt bring forth children, and thy desire shall be to thy husband, and he shall rule over thee.

Here, we see God's new plan for woman. She shall be sorrowful in childbirth and her husband shall rule over her. This was not God's original intent. Women were created as an equal to men. They were to rule over the Earth together, but because of Eve's disobedience, she went under the authority of her husband. His desires will be her desires. No longer were they in sync, both hearing from God as equal heirs of the blessing. After this, God rebuked Adam and gave him his consequence for disobedience.

> *And unto Adam, he said, Because thou hast hearkened unto the voice of thy wife. And has eaten of the tree, of which I commanded thee, saying, Thou shalt not eat of it: cursed is the ground for thy sake; in sorrow shalt, thou eat of it all the days of thy life. Also, Thorns and thistles shall it bring forth to thee; and thou shalt eat the herb of the field; In the sweat of thy face shalt thou eat bread, till thou return unto the ground; for out of it wast thou took: for dust thou art, and unto dust shalt thou return.*

So Adam was forced to labor in the Earth. He worked hard; the Earth produced thorns or things to disrupt his purpose and made it difficult for him to obtain the promise. Finally, Adam gave his wife, who was once a part of him, a name. Now that they had distance between them, she needed her name.

> *And Adam called his wife's name Eve; because she was the mother of all living. Unto Adam also and to his wife did the LORD God make coats of skins, and clothed them.*

What a stark contrast to the relationship man and woman had with God in the beginning! There was no separation between man and woman. They heard from God together. What one received, the other also received. There was no confusion. They were together, heard things together, did things together and had no reason to dispute. As soon as the woman stepped away, the serpent (the enemy) entered, brought confusion and ultimately, disobedience to God.

The purpose of a name

To understand the significance of a Sidechick being nameless, it is critical to establish the purpose of a name. As was seen in Genesis 3, God showed displeasure in their disobedience in the garden. He then spoke separately to man and woman for the first time and gave them each a consequence. Adam, knowing this separation, now identifies the woman as Eve or mother to all. Originally, in Genesis 2:23-24, Adam said:

> *This is now bone of my bones, and flesh of my flesh: she shall be called Woman because she was taken out of Man. Therefore shall a man leave his father and his mother, and shall cleave unto his wife: and they shall be one flesh.*

Being referred to as woman reflected Eve's origin and identity. She came from man and existed for the same purpose, therefore, maintaining his name.

A name identifies who you are and gives you purpose. Some parents give their children a name as soon as they conceive them. This means that they already had a particular purpose or plan for the child. They may be naming their child after a deceased family member or loved one. They may have had difficulty conceiving, and because of this, they named their children in the faith, expecting the fulfillment of the promise. Contrarily, some parents wait until the birth of the child before giving the child a name. They wait to look into the eyes of the child and be inspired by what they see. Either way, a name provides identity. In some cultures, the surname is given to recognize only the father, while in other cultures, it is custom to give two surnames, one for the father and the other for the mother.

Often, people who come from a mixed background or a family in which the parents have different cultures have a hard time choosing a name. They must decide whether to give an American name or a traditional name from their family's country. Many parents decide to use one for the first name and the other for the middle name. My husband and I decided to give our daughter a

Hebrew name that means princess. Her
middle name is a traditional American name.
We want her to understand who God has
called her to be, as well as the heritage in
which she was born.

Albeit, in American culture, people
don't take careful consideration in what they
name their children, in other cultures a name
is very significant. One day at the mall, my
daughter and I purchased a toy from a kiosk.
The young man selling the toy to us was an
Arab. When he saw my daughter, he asked
her what her name was. When she
responded, his face lit up with surprise. It
was as if he'd found a long lost cousin. He
repeated her name and asked frantically,
"Are you Arab? You're Arab?" I was shocked
that he would even think we could be Arab.
Sadly, I responded no. Then, he asked if I
knew what her name means. I explained that
I did and he was thrilled that he had found
someone who appeared to share, or at least,
appreciate his culture.

Thinking back, I realize that although we may not have looked Arab, having an Arab name was enough to convince him otherwise. When you give a name to someone or something in your life, that determines how you treat it, regardless of whether that's what it is or not. At the conclusion of Genesis 3, Adam gave his woman a name. She became Eve, mother of all living. There, he reestablished Eve's identity. She was to help Adam procure the blessing that God released upon them. However, she would no longer be equal, working alongside Adam. Instead, the woman would have her identity and function primarily as a mother. She would be subject to her husband and could not fulfill her calling outside of him.

As a Sidechick married to a visionary, you must be willing to give up your name. Rather than working and establishing your plans alone, you must be ready to plan and work with your husband. This could mean staying home to build a family, working to build a business or giving up your career to build a ministry. You may be working behind the scenes for years, and nobody ever knows your name. I can think of several wives who have been married to great men but are hardly ever in the spotlight. Does this mean they are insignificant? No. These women have worked tirelessly to make their husbands' work easier. They take on stress and bear the burden of big businesses without anyone ever knowing. This is especially true in the early years of a marriage where there are innumerable sacrifices that women make to build their husbands' visions. As a Sidechick, you may feel unsettled by the fact that you can't do all that you want to do. Just know that your sacrifices now will make way for you to be able to do whatever you desire to do later. God has big plans for you too. Giving up on your plans to establish those of your husband may only be a temporary sacrifice. Hang in there, keep building and God will bless you abundantly.

CHAPTER 4

Intercessor

They were getting ready for a holiday party. The servers were setting the tables. The valet service was putting up signs outside to show people where to park. The house was well lit, decorated from top to bottom and all ready for guests to arrive. Vashti was getting her hair and make-up done upstairs. Music filled the air and dishes clang together as the caterers made the final preparations.

"I hope everything goes well tonight," Vashti thought to herself. "I don't think I can deal with another argument."

Vashti had been married for several years now. It seemed like forever. There were extreme highs, for example, moving into a beautiful new home and terrible lows, for example, her husband's drinking. He occasionally drunk throughout the year, but the holidays were always terrible. He would drink for hours and start arguments about the smallest things like how she wore her hair that day or how clean the kitchen was left the night before. Sometimes, he would become so irate that she had to leave to get him to calm down. He was a total jerk when he was drunk, but very few people knew. He had managed to maintain his public persona, all the while, serving as governor.

Tonight, she just wanted to get through the party without an episode. She hoped he would limit his drinking since there were some influential people in attendance. But as the guests started arriving, she could hear her husband asking the servers for another drink every time they passed by. She was sure that this night would have a disastrous end. While her stylist finished her hair, she thought of a way to avoid the party.

"Maybe I'll pretend to be sick or get an emergency phone call from my mom about the

kids," she thought. "I just can't take this embarrassment anymore."

"Vashti!," she heard him yell, interrupting her thoughts. "Come down here and show my friends how beautiful you are!"

Sheer horror is what she felt. She couldn't believe he was doing this again. She was tired of the parading around and flaunting he always wanted her to do. She was tired of trying to impress people and make everyone think they had the perfect marriage. She was tired of being a trophy wife. She'd had enough. She didn't answer; she refused to go downstairs. He continued to call for her, but was met with no response. Finally, he came upstairs to see what the hold-up was. When he saw her sitting in the bathroom fully dressed, he commanded her to come downstairs. Again, she refused.

"I'm sick of you and this marriage," she finally said.

To her surprise, he yelled, "Then leave!" and walked back downstairs to the party.

As soon as he left, Vashti couldn't believe her ears. With tears in her eyes, she packed her belongings into an overnight bag and tip-toed down the back stairway and out the door to the garage. That night, she drove away for the last time.

This is like the beginning of the story of Queen Esther. I believe she was one of the greatest intercessors to walk the Earth. If you don't know her story, I will provide a brief synopsis here. However, I encourage you to do a more in-depth study on your own. From studying Esther, we can learn so much about the qualities of being a Sidechick. In this chapter, we will focus on her grace as an intercessor.

Esther 1 begins by telling us about King Ahasuerus. He ruled over one hundred provinces from India to Ethiopia. This man had great power but appeared to lack good character. We learn that he threw a party for over one hundred days and showed off his wealth. He invited all kinds of people to join him in this elaborate celebration. They played music and drank wine to each man's contentment. Esther 1:7-8 says:

> And they gave them drink in vessels of gold, (the vessels being diverse one from another,) and royal wine in abundance, according to the state of the king.
> And the drinking was according to the law; none did compel: for so the king had appointed to all the officers of his house, that they should do according to every man's pleasure.

After the king was drunk, he sent his chamberlains to bring his wife, Vashti, to the party. The Bible describes a separate party that Queen Vashti threw simultaneously for the women. This would imply that the men were separated from the women. The king called for Queen Vashti to come show off her beauty, but she refused. The king became furious. He was also likely embarrassed in front of the other men at the party. The story continues to unfold as the king's trusted advisers explained what the king should do. According to Esther 1:19, one man said:

> *"That Vashti comes no more before king Ahasuerus, and let the king give her royal estate unto another that is better than she."*

This man was advising King Ahasuerus to put away Queen Vashti for her refusal to obey his commands. He advised the king to replace her with someone better.

One may argue that Queen Vashti was justified in her refusal to parade herself in front of a crowd of drunk men. She may have been subject to sneers, inappropriate stares or touching. Most women do not want to be put on display outside of their control. However, Queen Vashti's refusal to obey her husband had more severe consequences. One consequence is that she jeopardized the king's public image. The second consequence is that she negatively influenced the women in the kingdom around her.

The first consequence we will discuss is the king's public image. Because Vashti was married to the king, she was expected to obey his commands like everyone else. Unfortunately, she did not have the luxury of separating home life from her life "in office" or as royalty. She could not separate her role as a wife from her role as queen. I know firsthand what it is like to live with someone who has high-ranking authority outside of the home. There have been many times when I've received severe correction at home relating to my position or job in ministry. My first reaction was to feel unloved as a wife. However, I had to realize that the correction was for my position and was unrelated to the love we share as husband and wife. Instead of biting back and feeling attacked, I had to take the correction and grow like every other servant leader in the ministry. Regardless of how Queen Vashti felt about her husband as a man, she had a responsibility as the queen to obey him.

When you are married to a man with high-ranking authority, your image does matter. I struggled with putting much effort into my appearance for a long time. It wasn't just what I wore, but how I wore it, or not just being happy, but also appearing to be satisfied. My husband used to always ask me what was wrong. I could not understand why he thought I was upset. I have always considered myself a happy and easy-going person. Conversely, I tend to maintain a straight face. Some people may take this as me being mean and unapproachable. This does not mean that I couldn't be myself, but I had to be mindful of how others perceived me. All throughout my days and weeks, I have to interact with strangers. Therefore, it was important for me to adjust for the sake of our image. I had to intentionally make sure I was smiling because it wasn't enough for me to just be happy, I had to show it. In addition to my appearance affecting my image, my impression also changed my husband's image.

People are looking at the wife to determine the greatness of a man. The Bible explains it this way in 1 Corinthians 11:7:

> *For a man indeed ought not to cover his head, forasmuch as he is the image and glory of God: but the woman is the glory of the man.*

It is essential for every wife to remember that she not only represents herself, but she also describes her husband. While you are single, your responsibility is to represent Christ. The way people view the king is based on the appearance of the queen, who is his glory. To be the glory of someone means that you add honor to them. When we give the glory and honor to God, we say that we are because of Him. When we are well manicured, peaceful, kind and well dressed, we are saying that our husband (or our God) takes good care of us. We communicate to others through our appearance and attitude that all of our needs are met, and we are abundantly blessed. Have you ever seen a couple where the man was unattractive or disheveled, but the wife was beautiful? This happens all the time. Even an unsaved man knows he needs to make sure his wife looks good. People will judge him on how his wife carries herself. Having a fine wife adds credibility and significance to him. Now, think about this. Have you ever seen a couple in which the man was impeccably dressed, and the woman was in shambles? It's not likely. If you do, that tells you something about their relationship. This could be a sign of abuse, control or insecurity. A man who is insecure may not want people to be drawn to his wife. He may believe that if she is attractive, another man may take her away from him. A wife who is not cared for may also indicate a controlling or abusive man. Think of pimps who are always well-dressed and sporting expensive cars. Then think about the prostitutes who are controlled by them. They are usually ill-dressed and never sporting their cars. The pimp usually does not let the woman out of his sight for too long. She doesn't receive enough time or money to make sure she looks beautiful. This is an abusive and controlling relationship. The pimp feels that having multiple women brings him credibility. He is not aware of the fact that one loved, well-taken care of woman would bring him all the glory he needs.

The king's public image and how other people saw him was everything. In 1 Timothy 3:4-5, we see instructions for every man wanting the title of bishop in the church.

> One that ruleth well his own house, having his children in subjection with all gravity;(For if a man know not how to rule his own house, how shall he take care of the church of God?)

This applies, not only to men who want to serve as bishops but to any man who wants to have credibility. You can replace the phrase "how shall he take care of the house of God" with "how can he run a fortune five hundred company" or "how can he lead a professional basketball team?" Imagine if the word had gotten out about Queen Vashti not following the king's commands. How would anyone respect the king if he couldn't even get his wife to obey him? I want to challenge you to have the appearance and attitude of Christ at all times. It is not easy to maintain your composure when you are dealing with difficult circumstances. However, you must allow God to guide your words and actions so that you will be a reflection of Him.

The second consequence that Queen Vashti's actions had was the potential it had to influence other women negatively. The other men at the party hastily offered advice to King Ahasuerus because his decision would ultimately affect their families as well. As the king's trusted advisers, they had a responsibility to think about the impact Vashti's behavior had on the entire kingdom. If other women heard about Queen Vashti disobeying her husband, they would follow her lead. Specifically, one adviser to the king says in Esther 1:20-22:

> *Then when the king's edict is proclaimed throughout all his vast realm, all the women will respect their husbands, from the least to the greatest.*
> *He sent dispatches to all parts of the kingdom, to each province in its script and each people in their language, proclaiming that every man should be ruler over his household, using his native tongue.*

It was important that the decree was sent to every household, even in various languages. The king wanted it to be clear that men ruled their households and those women were to obey their husbands. No matter the rank of the husband in society, women were in subjection to their husbands. If any woman even thought about stepping out of line, she was reminded that she could face the same consequences as Queen Vashti. Someone, more fit would replace her.

Women who marry great men are always in the spotlight. What we do has ripple effects because it models how other women should behave. Queen Vashti's obedience was not just for her, but for everyone watching. She served as a model for every single woman waiting and preparing to be married, and not only single women, other wives as well. Whether you want to or not, your life is a pattern after which many women will form their lives. Most of this may go unsaid, but trust me, it is happening. This is both a great honor and a humbling reality for us to face. The fact is that God chose you to be a wife and to make known His excellency through your relationship.

The Bible does not give detail as to why Queen Vashti refused to come at the call of the King. What we do know is that she was beautiful and her husband wanted to show her off to his friends. It was customary in this culture and time for women to entertain men at parties. However, I can understand why Queen Vashti would refuse. She was in the middle of her party, entertaining her guests and the men were extremely drunk. I can imagine any woman being uncomfortable in this situation. However, I believe Queen Vashti missed an opportunity to intercede.

To intercede means to intervene on behalf of another. To mediate or intermediate between two parties. A Sidechick has the responsibility to intercede for her husband at all times. At the beginning of this book, we talked about how God created woman to support man. Remember these words can be translated more accurately to mean an *ezer, k'enegdo* or savior counterpart. Sidechicks must stand in the gap in the same manner that our Savior took on our sins. In 2 Corinthians 5:21, we are reminded: *For our sake he made him be sin who knew no sin so that in him we might become the righteousness of God.*

King Ahasuerus had a sin problem. He drunk excessively and flaunted his wealth. Vashti should have been praying for him day and night. Since we don't know for sure, let's suppose for a brief moment that she was praying for her husband. She could have grown tired of praying and not seeing any changes. An intercessor must not grow weary when there are no visible results. If we stopped praying every time we did not see what we were praying for, we would never pray. Queen Vashti also could have been praying silent prayers, but behaving in a way that did not reflect her faith in God. The Bible says in 1 Corinthians 7:14-16:

> *For the unbelieving husband is sanctified by the wife, and the husband sanctifies the skeptical wife: else were your children unclean, but now are they holy. But if the unbelieving depart, let him depart. A brother or a sister is not under bondage in such cases: but God hath called us to peace. For what knowest thou, O wife, whether thou*

shalt save thy husband? Or how knowest thou, O man, whether thou shalt save thy wife?

Often, we hear this scripture and think that the spouse simply brought the other spouse to church and he or she got saved. However, what we fail to recognize is that by being faithful, kind, and loving to your unbelieving spouse, he may desire to know more about the Jesus you serve. But, if you constantly disobey, nag, yell and stress your unsaved spouse, what kind of God does your character bear witness of? Is this a Jesus who an unsaved person would want to follow? Probably not. Our actions speak louder than any words we could ever say.

Imagine if Queen Vashti obeyed the king and came down to parade herself in front of the drunk men and then, went back and prayed with tear-filled eyes for her husband to be delivered. When we obey our husbands, we obey God. When we honor our husbands, we honor God. Let me be clear that this is not meant to encourage you to marry a drug dealer, nor should you engage in illegal activity just because your husband engages in it. What I'm saying is that when you discern something disrupting your family, don't let it end your marriage. Instead, you should take up your armor and engage in a spiritual fight! Don't allow a struggle your husband is facing to be the end of your marriage. Pray to God and ask for wisdom on how to deal with the problem. You have sacrificed your time, money and life for this marriage, and you shouldn't let it go without a fight. Prayer is your weapon. Ephesians 6:12 reminds us:

> *For we wrestle not against flesh and blood, but against principalities, against powers, against the rulers of the darkness of this world, against spiritual wickedness in high places.*

Every fight, disagreement and strife between you and your spouse is designed to break up your marriage. The enemy knows that he has no chance against a healthy marriage. Through our unions, we legalize our seed to bruise the enemy's head, according to Genesis 2. Through strong marriages, we produce more people who have authority over the enemy. We build generations who know God and follow His commandments. As an intercessor, this is what you are protecting. If you don't get anything else from this chapter, know that your marriage is worth fighting for it. The people, communities, organizations and generations that will be blessed by your marriage extend beyond what you can see. Your marriage is worth fighting for it.

An older lady once shared with me that she and her husband disagreed about tithing. Before getting married, she was an adamant tither and gave to the church as often as she could. When she got married, she discovered her husband did not believe in giving so much to the church. He told her he did not want to tithe. Instead of outright disobeying her husband or making it a source of contention, she obeyed her husband. She prayed that God would know her heart and work on her husband's faith. She continued to give to the church consistently, although in smaller amounts than she wanted to give. Eventually, those amounts became larger and larger, and one day, her husband came on board with tithing. Although he still had his doubts, he saw the faithfulness of God in their lives and allowed her to tithe.

I am a consistent tither, and even from a young age, I had no problem giving to the church. When I first got married and my husband and I went to church together, I asked my husband how much he wanted to give. I would have been outraged if he told me not to give or to give an amount smaller than my tithes and offering. However, I knew that marriage meant submission one to another. It wasn't enough for me to know God's desire for us to give tithes and offerings. I had to be on one accord with my husband. Fortunately, he told me to give what I was planning to give. What a sigh of relief. Since then, he has relinquished most financial planning and control to me. Even with his blessing, I still submit to his authority. I believe my early revelation of my responsibility to submit gave him the confidence that I would follow the leading of the Holy Spirit.

Some women make the mistake of dealing with issues in marriage by insisting on being right. When you have a revelation that your husband does not have, it is not your responsibility to get him to see things your way. There are many areas where I felt like I knew more than my husband. I had some experiences and responsibilities that he simply did not have. When we got married, I had graduated college, worked full time and purchased a home. He was still pursuing his undergraduate degree and working part-time. There were many times when we would disagree with decisions that we needed to make. Sometimes, I felt like I knew the best move to make because I had experience in a particular area. When he would decide for the family, I often didn't respond to allow God to help me surrender my will. I had to pray and ask God to help me and to cover our marriage. My prayers often sounded like this. *Lord, I think this is a crazy idea. I don't believe that this will turn out for our good, but I trust you. I trust that you speak to my husband and that you will see this through. Lord, honor me for my submission. God help my unbelief. In Jesus' name. Amen.* After those prayers, my husband would sometimes have second thoughts and ask me what I thought before following through with the original decision. More often, the decision would yield miraculous results.

The more I submitted to my husband and interceded for him, the more confidence and wisdom my husband could use and operate with me. Imagine if every time he was going to make a decision, I was right there complaining and voicing my skepticism. He would lose enthusiasm and the ability to grow in wisdom. Just like with

Noah, God speaks to your husband in ways that he does not speak to you. It is your husband's duty from God, not yours, to communicate the vision for your family.

Your responsibility is to submit to your husband and then intercede on his behalf. You don't always have to be a cheerleader, but you should do more cheering than chastising. I believe this is one reason successful men leave the women who started with them before they were famous. Another woman comes along who didn't have to make any sacrifices and witness the husband's early mistakes. All she does is cheer the man on without judgment or the memory of his failures. Sometimes, just the presence of the wife makes him relive his mistakes. Other times, it is the woman's inability to encourage her husband after all of the mediation. It takes an incredible amount of prayer and forgiveness (we will discuss this later) to recover and move forward in your marriage. While you are interceding, God will give you strategy and insight. He will tell you when to intervene and when to be quiet. He will provide open space for you to gain influence in the eyes of your husband. Let's continue our story of Esther.

After listening to the suggestions of a few trusted advisers at the party, King Ahasuerus followed through with removing Vashti from the throne. He then placed a call for fair young virgins to audition for her crown. This is where we are introduced to Esther. Esther 2 tells us about the process for young virgins to have an opportunity to come into the royal palace.

Once King Ahasereus called for the young virgins in his search for Queen Vashti's replacement, Esther joined the race. There was a year-long process that all the women had to undergo before they were ready to see the king. During this time, the women were stripped of their old clothes, languages and relationships. They lived in quarters with maidens and bathed in various oils and perfumes. The oils were for purification. After a year, the king called for Esther to visit with him. She was beautiful and humble, and quickly found favor with the king. He decided to make Esther his new queen.

During Esther's time in the palace, a crooked royal assistant tricked the king into issuing a decree against all the Jews. This decision would exile Esther, her uncle and all the other Jews in the nation. Being of Jewish heritage, Esther had something personal on the line. Now she, like the previous queen, Vashti, had an opportunity to intercede.

The law restricted Esther from going to see the king on her own. She certainly could not demand to see the king and tell him why the decree he'd issued was a terrible idea. I believe God gave Esther a divine strategy that would protect her identity and save an entire nation of Jews. The story continues with Esther having her uncle to gather all the Jews in the city together to fast for three days. At the end of the three days, Esther approached the inner court of the king with the hope that he would extend his gold scepter to her. This would indicate that the king was willing to see her and it was okay for her to approach. Even after making it this far, Esther waited for the perfect time to voice her request. Over the next day, God orchestrated the perfect plan for Esther to intercede on behalf of the Jews.

Esther's ability to be patient and not act hastily turned her intercession into influence. As a woman, you influence men. You need to use this influence to ensure the plans of God are established, not to have things go your way. In Esther 6 and 7, we see how Esther uses her position to plan a dinner and expose the wicked assistant. The king is extremely displeased and issues another decree to override his previous one. Esther uses her petition to save an entire nation of Jews.

How the intercessor is changed

Intercession is not just about the person or thing you are praying for to be changed. When the intercessor prays, they are also transformed. When you intercede for someone else, you take on the other person's situation and put yourself in their shoes. The Bible says in 2 Corinthians 5:21:

> *For he hath made him be sin for us, who knew no sin; that we might be made the righteousness of God in him.*

Jesus took our place on the cross. He became sin so that we would be made righteous through Him. He took the blame and the punishment that we deserved. As a wife, it is easy to be frustrated when things don't go your way. It is also easy to complain when your husband makes a mistake. But I believe when you think of all the things you have done wrong and how Jesus gave His life to ensure your salvation, you will change your attitude.

Taking on the responsibility of intercessor in your marriage reminds you of your significance and the importance of your marriage. When problems or challenges arise, don't see yourself as a victim, see yourself as an intercessor. Let your relationship with Jesus Christ guide you through this challenging process. Romans 8:34 says, "*Who is he that condemneth? It is Christ that died, yea rather, that is risen again, who is even at the right hand of God, who also maketh intercession for us.*"

As a Sidechick, let it be your husband's testimony that you consistently make intercession for him and your family.

Chapter 5

Loyal

There once lived a man who was married and had two sons. They lived a good life. Then, one year, everything changed. There was a terrible wildfire in their hometown that burned up most of that year's crop. Farmers were struggling to reap any harvest and people did not have an adequate food supply. So, the man decided to take his wife and sons to live in another town.

After moving to the new town, the husband suddenly died, and the woman was left alone with her two sons. The sons grew older, got married, each to a beautiful wife, and built a wonderful home together. The woman, her sons and their wives lived together for many years. Suddenly, the two sons died, and the woman was now left without her husband and her two sons. She thought God had surely turned away from her.

After everything she had lost, the woman decided to go to a place where she could find help. This was a place that showed kindness to widows and would allow her to die in peace. She told her daughters-in-law that it would be best for them to go back to their families and prepare to one day remarry. But the daughter-in-laws refused. The woman insisted that they return to their homes because she had nothing to offer them. One daughter-in-law agreed and went back to her mother's house. The other one refused to leave and declared that she would stay with the mother-in-law until death. Seeing that this particular daughter-in-law was intent on staying with her, the woman set off on another journey.

When they arrived at the new town, the woman gave her daughter-in-law some specific instructions. She told her to go to a large farm nearby and ask if she could collect the leftover crops. The daughter-in-law did precisely as she was told and worked from sun-up to sun-down. When the owner of the field returned to check on the harvest, he inquired about the new worker. His assistants explained that the young woman had asked to reap crops behind the servants and that she had worked all day. Very pleased, the owner gave her extra food to eat and water to drink. He also sent her home with enough food for later. After a short while, the owner married the woman and together, they had a son. The mother-in-law continued living with them and cared for the child, and the family lived happily ever after.

A modern interpretation of the story of Naomi and Ruth

So many women are looking for Boaz, but how many women are developing themselves as Ruth? If you study the book of Ruth, I believe you will find courage and hope. What I also discovered is a call to be loyal. Throughout this chapter, I will discuss this Sidechick quality that Ruth possessed. I will also provide a brief synopsis of the book of Ruth to build my case.

One scripture that comes to mind when thinking about Ruth is 1 Corinthians 15:58 which says:

> *Therefore, my beloved brethren, be ye steadfast, unmovable, always abounding in the work of the Lord, forasmuch as ye know that your labour is not in vain in the Lord.*

The three qualities that I want to expound upon from this verse are steadfast, immovable and always abounding in the work of the Lord.

Ruth embodied each one of these characteristics, and for this reason, she became part of one of the most touching love stories ever written.

Steadfast

What does it mean to be steadfast? To be steadfast means to be loyal. It means to be faithful, committed, dedicated and firm. Since you have made a covenant, every wife needs to be committed. However, as a Sidechick, your commitment goes beyond that. You are committed, not just to your husband, but also to his vision. You agree that for better or worse, you will be there to help actualize the vision. Steadfast goes beyond just staying in your marriage. Some people stay in a marriage to keep others from looking down on them, while others stay married for the money, but to be steadfast means you have your mind set on what you are trying to accomplish. You don't waver in your commitment. You are not in one moment and out the next. Your husband can trust fully in you and knows that you are on his side.

For a man on a mission, a loyal woman is a dream come true. There are enough pressures associated with being a visionary, therefore, worrying about if his wife is really with him should not be added to the list.

Unmovable

Unmovable means that you are still. It is amazing to me how many people threaten or even talk about divorce in their marriages. This brings on unnecessary amounts of stress and division between husbands and wives. I have heard many couples agree not to bring up divorce in an argument, but once the idea is in someone's head, you can never erase it. If you know the person you love is considering leaving you, you will always be on high alert. You can't relax, put your guards down and enjoy one another. Every time there is a disagreement, your mind will replay the moment your spouse said he would leave you. Put your husband at ease. I am not saying to be naïve if there are problems, but there are healthy ways to deal with issues. Be respectful in disagreements and work through your problems together. Always remember that you are on the same team. Build each other up so you can win.

The book of Ruth starts out with a sorrowful story of how three women became widows. It all started when there was a famine in the land that killed a woman named Naomi's husband. She was left with her two sons. They found wives, one of which was Ruth. After ten years, both sons died, leaving the three women as widows. After mourning their losses, Naomi blessed and dismissed her former daughters-in-law, telling them to return to their native land. She advised them to find other husbands while they are still young, but Ruth refused to leave.

> *And Ruth said, Intreat me not to leave thee, or to return from following after thee: for whither thou goest, I will go; and where thou lodgest, I will lodge: thy people shall be my people, and thy God my God. Ruth 1:21-22*

Naomi, her mother-in-law, obliged and they went about life together. Ruth stuck by Naomi's side and did everything she was told to do. It is through this loyalty and following that Ruth obtained the blessing. She was found by Boaz while working in the field as her mother-in-law instructed her to do. Likewise, throughout the rest of the story, Naomi gave Ruth specific instructions. Ruth was faithful in following those instructions and obtained favor from Boaz. He made sure Ruth had food to eat every day and all of her needs were met.

When the circumstances get difficult, will you stay around or will you leave? To be true means to show firm or continuous support to a person or thing. Loyalty does not differentiate between how well the person or thing is doing. A loyal fan will cheer hysterically in the fourth quarter with ten seconds left, even if their favorite team is losing by twenty points. A loyal friend will be around, whether you are having a good day or a bad one.

Likewise, for a loyal spouse, there are no storms strong enough to change your position. Your confession should continue to be, "I will remain by my husband's side." Galatians 5:22 says, *"But the fruit of the Spirit is love, joy, peace, longsuffering, gentleness, goodness, faith."* Long-suffering means that you show patience even when your problem is someone else's fault. You show patience with your husband in the midst of every mistake he makes. Forgive and remain understanding and kind throughout the process. Ephesians 4:2 says, *"With all lowliness and meekness, with longsuffering, forbearing one another in love."* This means that we must humble ourselves, be patient and be forgiving. When you think your spouse deserves the silent treatment, pray for the strength to love him instead. Start by remembering the mistakes you've made and how God forgave you. You don't deserve forgiveness, but God forgives you anyway. You will face challenges in your marriage. Know that your marriage is greater than any trial you may face.

Ruth's predicament was not her fault. She didn't ask to be a widow. She also didn't ask to be left in a foreign land, but she remained loyal. It was almost as if Ruth had the revelation that her service was for a greater purpose. She may have come from an idolatrous family, but after being married, she experienced God through her mother-in-law. This brings me to the last dimension of Ruth's loyalty: always abounding in the work of the Lord.

The work of the Lord

Eddie Foster, in his article *Fruit of the Spirit,* says, "Longsuffering is enduring trials and waiting patiently and faithfully for God's intervention." Ruth must have known about the power and love of God. Although her family worshipped other gods, she had the revelation that God is faithful. The first time her mother-in-law implores her to leave, Ruth says:

> *Intreat me not to leave thee, or to*
> *return from following after thee: for*

whither thou goest, I will go; and where thou lodgest, I will lodge: thy people shall be my people, and thy God my God.

I imagine that Ruth had seen God perform miracles for them. A group of women who lost their sole providers would need the provision of God to survive. In those times, women relied on their husbands for everything. They usually didn't work outside of the home in the manner we are used to now, but God had been good through every season. Ruth probably watched Naomi endure these trails with grace and faith in God. She had found someone to model her life after. If Naomi, a woman who had lost her husband and sons, could keep pressing forward, Ruth found encouragement that allowed her to move forward as well. When Ruth's sister-in-law went back to her country, Ruth had another opportunity to leave, but she remained to carry out the work of the Lord. When many people use trials to deny God, Ruth used her trial to build her faith in God.

The Bible says to serve as unto the Lord. When you are serving, it is important to remember to do it as unto the Lord. Whether on a job, in your home or your church, your service is ultimately for God. When your supervisor is rude and treats you poorly, remember to continue working as unto the Lord. In this litigious age, people are quick to file a complaint, quit and sue people who mistreat them. I am fully aware that serious issues come up in the workplace that justifies a person doing these things, but more often, a person would lead people to Christ if he or she remained loyal and served as unto the Lord.

In your marriage, you must remember that you bring glory to God by serving your husband. You may be tired, annoyed and frustrated, but your sacrifice for the vision is a blessing to God. This revelation should make you honored to serve your husband. Most times, I am miserable washing dishes and cleaning our home. However, I must remember to thank God for His faithfulness and the honor to serve in this capacity. I can imagine that Ruth got tired, had moments of disbelief and wanting to quit, but she kept going, knowing that all things would work together for her good. She followed everything her mother-in-law instructed her to do. God was at work all throughout her service.

Traditionally, a man's brother would take care of his wife in the event of his death. Unfortunately for Ruth and Naomi, both of Naomi's sons died. While Ruth was working in a field, she had no idea that this set into motion a plan that would take care of her for the rest of her life. This field belonged to a wealthy man named Boaz. He was a relative of Naomi, pretty much like a distant cousin. Once Boaz found out who Ruth was and that she was also living with her mother-in-law, he made it his responsibility to care for her. Eventually, he fell in love with Ruth, and they got married. They had a child named Obed, who was the father of Jesse, the father of David. It is from this lineage that Jesus Christ was born. What an awesome testament to the faithfulness of God! Your loyalty could be the tool God is using to set up provision for your marriage and your family. Working to help your husband fulfill a vision is not just for you, but for many generations to come. Find inspiration to keep working, knowing that you are abounding in the work of the Lord. Like Ruth, your loyalty will unlock divine protection and provision for you and your family.

CHAPTER 6

Creative & Resourceful

Proverbs 31 is one of the most referenced scriptures in the Bible when preparing single women to be wives. However, this passage isn't just about being a good wife, after all, stories of good wives can be found all over the Bible. What Proverbs 31 describes are examples of expert homemakers. What Proverbs 31 shows us is the epitome of an entrepreneurial wife. Starting at verse 10, it reads:

> Who can find a virtuous woman? For her price is far above rubies.
> The heart of her husband doth safely trust in her so that he shall not need spoil.
> She will do him good and not evil all the days of her life.

The woman described in Proverbs 31 has value beyond what any man can afford to pay. This is why the author states, "*Who can find a virtuous woman?*" Only God can give a man the revelation and favor to obtain a woman of this caliber. When a man does find a wife, according to Proverbs 18:22, *he finds a good thing and obtains favor from the Lord.* A man with this type of wife can trust her to do good for him and ensure all his needs are met. Verse 13 continues by describing her work ethic.

> *She seeketh wool, and flax, and worketh willingly with her hands.*
> *She is like the merchants' ships; she bringeth her food from afar.*
> *She riseth also while it is yet night, and giveth meat to her household, and a portion to her maidens.*
> *She considereth a field, and buyeth it: with the fruit of her hands she planteth a vineyard.*
> *She girdeth her loins with strength, and strengtheneth her arms.*

She perceiveth that her merchandise is good: her candle goeth not out by night. She layeth her hands to the spindle, and her hands hold the distaff.

This woman works day and night. She is looking for bargains to help her family save money. She starts businesses and works them herself, ensuring they produce good fruit. She works to provide for her family, but also to give generously to those in need.

She stretcheth out her hand to the poor; yea, she reacheth forth her hands to the needy.
She is not afraid of the snow for her household: for all her household are clothed with scarlet.
She maketh herself coverings of tapestry; her clothing is silk and purple.

Serving others does not destroy her relationship with her family. She can make clothes for her household and still have leftovers to bless others. Her image is untainted among the people for her husband's sake. She is married to a man of great stature, but represents him well in deed and in character.

> *Her husband is known in the gates when he sitteth among the elders of the land.*
> *She maketh fine linen, and selleth it; and delivereth girdles unto the merchant.*
> *Strength and honour are her clothing, and she shall rejoice in time to come.*
> *She openeth her mouth with wisdom, and in her tongue is the law of kindness.*
> *She looketh well to the ways of her household, and eateth not the bread of idleness.*

She speaks out when she can add value to the conversation. She guards her words with care. She is not sitting around being catered to, but is continuously productive. She finds ways to make money and does not waste time. Her family takes notice of her hard work and kindness.

> Her children arise up, and call her blessed; her husband also, and he praiseth her.
> Many daughters have done virtuously, but thou excellent them all.
> Favor is deceitful, and beauty is vain: but a woman that feareth the LORD, she shall be praised.

Her secret to success is not in her beauty. Instead, her reverence of the Lord provides all that she needs. She will see the fruit of her labor and receive praise for her deeds.

> Give her of the fruit of her hands, and let her works praise her in the gates.

Homemakers may not be looked upon favorably in society, but the Bible esteems them as virtuous and priceless women. Reality television shows have reduced homemakers to women who go to brunch, engage in cat fights and spend up their husbands' money. These shows promote laziness, excessive concern with the outward appearance and haughtiness. But homemakers are women of class and grace. They take care of their children, spend wisely and conduct themselves with wisdom and kindness. True homemakers are entrepreneurs who take what they have and grow it for the glory of God. They are creative, inventive and wise. They bring glory to their husbands and God. Their husbands can trust them to do what is right. They don't have to worry about being embarrassed by their wives in public or about lacking any of their daily needs. They know that their wives will make sure they have everything they need, including food, clothes, shelter, provision and wisdom, just to name a few. A great man needs an entrepreneurial wife to grow and establish his vision.

I use the word vision often to describe the purpose and plan of God. It is so critical to marry a man with a vision to establish a plan for your life. If you go into anything without a plan, you will surely fail. There is no guarantee that you will succeed with a plan, but at least if you fail, you know how and where to begin again.

There are so many examples of men and women who do business together. Bill and Melinda Gates, Will and Jada Smith, Barack and Michelle Obama, for example, have built incredible empires together. They are power teams, conquering whatever they have been tasked to do with force and focus. In each case, if the man had the vision, the woman worked tirelessly alongside him to bring the vision to pass. The woman had to deal with the infrastructure and behind the scenes aspects of the ventures. The wife could not just sit on the sidelines and watch her husband try to bring it to pass. She had a critical role in building from the very beginning. Without her support and work, I'm convinced the vision would not be possible.

When we started our ministry, and to this day, my husband remains the face of the ministry. He is on flyers, stands in front of the congregation to preach and teach, and carries the bulk of the public appearances. I, on the other hand, handle the business aspects of the ministry and try to build infrastructure to make his job easier. I am behind the scenes, but a part of what God is doing with my husband's vision. I also continue to work and build a brand that provides for our family.

I don't understand stay-at-home moms who don't help the husband with the vision. This help may come in different forms. For instance, some may help by being directly involved in building the business. Others may help by taking care of the home matters so that the husband can devote maximum attention to the vision.

Some women leave their kids with nannies or drop them off at school so they can hang out and have fun. They relegate the cooking and cleaning to home servants and use their time to spend money. I have no problem with paying for home services; I do as much as I can do, but if you have the time and choose not to use it to help your husband build the vision, you are the problem. The Bible says a virtuous woman is not given to idleness. This means you are not sitting around being unproductive. On the contrary, you seek ways to be productive. Ultimately, the vision will be a blessing to your entire family, so wives have a stake in making sure it is fulfilled.

Women often have a unique gift of making something out of nothing. In the very beginning of your marriage, you may find that you don't have everything you need or want. The vision is most likely in its infant stage. You may take a thought and build it into a business, or you may take a small business and build it into an enterprise. Whatever you are given, don't be dismayed by small beginnings. Pray that God gives you creativity and strategies to make something out of nothing. Like the woman described in Proverbs 31, you can find ways to make sure your family is well taken care of. You may turn a hobby into a small source of income, or you may learn to sew so that you can save on clothing and home décor costs. Then again, you may need to coupon to save money to buy a home. You may even take classes or go back to school to learn a skill necessary to grow your endeavor. You are built with ingenuity and designed to take care of your household.

Regardless of how you contribute to the vision, know that you are an invaluable asset. Whether you are in front or behind the scenes, what you do matters. In a divorce, it is common for couples to argue over who gets what. I have heard of wealthy couples splitting multi-million dollar businesses 50/50. The public is often outraged if the wife gets half of a man's business. What people fail to realize is that the wife most likely had a hand in the work and sacrifice that went into the business early on. So, although she may not be well-known or seen, she plays a vital role in the company and is due to her fair cut. My prayer is that God blesses you with a long, loving and fruitful marriage.

CHAPTER 7

Faith

There was an old lady who lived with her aging husband. They had tried for many years, but couldn't seem to have children. Now, long past child-bearing age, they counted it as a loss. The wife brought up the idea of using a surrogate, and the husband agreed. They were sure that this would solve the problem and provide a child to inherit their estate. So, they proceeded on with finding a surrogate mother to carry his child. They found a woman willing to be the surrogate and invited her to live in their house. For nine months, the wife watched as the surrogate mother's belly expanded and her husband's affection toward her grew.

After the child was born, everyone, including her husband, began to spoil the child and comfort the mother. As the young child grew older, there was an evident rift between the wife, the surrogate mother and the child. The wife could not take it anymore and decided to take out the child's mother. She no longer wanted her in the picture because she reminded her of her barrenness. So, the wife made the young woman and her child leave their home.

Not long before this, an old friend had come to visit the husband and reminded him of the prophecy they'd received some time ago regarding God giving them a child of their own. The husband entertained the guest while the wife mocked them in private.

"Me? Have a child?" She laughed to herself at the thought. Just then, the old friend asked about the wife. The husband called for her to come into the living room. Reluctantly, she joined them for an afternoon snack.

> *"How have you been, Sarah?" asked the visitor.*
> *"Just fine. Had to deal with a few changes, but we're all good."*

"Are you sure?" He persisted. "I remember how intent you all were on having a child. You prayed, fasted, and even prepared for some time. After that, you all just kind of fell off the map. I didn't hear from you or speak to you for years. What happened to your faith?"

Sarah couldn't believe her ears. How could he insult her faith? He had no idea what she and her husband had been through. Years of trying to conceive, public humiliation and disappointment, to name a few.

"We still have faith. Just not for children. Our time has come and gone. God is still good."
"Okay, I just don't want you both to give up. If God said it, you should believe it. God is faithful."
"Thank you for the reminder," the husband said. "I guess we have given up and tried to do things on our own. But God has never failed us."

They continued in much lighter conversation. Later, the guest thanked them for their hospitality and left. The husband and wife went to bed, and for the first time in months, had intercourse. Nine months later, they had a new baby boy and named him Isaac, which means to laugh.

Faith to Follow

In the story of Abraham and Sarah, we see laughter in two significant moments. The first moment is in Genesis 17 when the Lord appears to Abraham and establishes His covenant between them.

> *And I [the Lord] will bless her [Sarah], and give thee a son also of her: yea, I will bless her, and she shall be a mother of nations; kings of people shall be of her. Then Abraham fell upon his face, and laughed, and said in his heart, Shall a child be born unto him that is a hundred years old? And shall Sarah, that is ninety years old, bear? And Abraham said unto God, O that Ishmael*

*might live before thee! And God said,
Sarah thy wife shall take thee a son
indeed; and thou shalt call his name
Isaac: and I will establish my covenant
with him for an everlasting covenant,
and with his seed after him.*

The second time we see laughter in the story of Abraham and Sarah is in Genesis 18. This time, it is Sarah doing the laughing. While in the tent, three angels appeared before Abraham. He instructed Sarah to go and prepare food for their guests. That's when the angels told Abraham that within a year's time, the Lord would give Sarah a son. Sarah, from the doors of the tent, heard what they said.

*Therefore Sarah laughed within herself,
saying, After I am waxed old shall I
have pleasure, my lord being old also?
And the Lord said unto Abraham;
Wherefore did Sarah laugh, saying,
Shall I of a surety bear a child, which
am old? Is anything too hard for*

the LORD? At the time appointed I will return unto thee, according to the time of life, and Sarah shall have a son. Then Sarah denied, saying, I laughed not; for she was afraid. And he said, Nay; but thou didst laugh.

From first glance, it would be easy to say that Abraham and Sarah just didn't believe God, but their responses are a little deeper than that. It is important to have context about their situation before diagnosing Abraham and Sarah's laughter. Likewise, when people look at your marriage, they have no idea what you have been through. People are quick to tell you what you should do, how to do it and when, but they don't know the years of struggle, hard work and sacrifice you've made, nor do they know the word of God for your marriage. You can read a good relationship book or get advice from a friend, but the word of the Lord is what matters in the end. With that, let's start with understanding when God calls Abram.

In Genesis 11, we meet Terah, Abram's father. Terah had taken Abram, Lot and Sarai from Ur and was on the way to Canaan, the promised land. They were from Ur, and everything they owned and everyone they knew was there, but they went anyway. Haran, Abram's brother, had already died, leaving his son, Lot, to their care. On the way to Canaan, Terah, Abram's father also died. Abram found himself between where he'd started and his promise. There is uncertainty about what their future holds, and they have lost people along the way, but God doesn't leave them there. In Genesis 12:1-4, the Lord says to Abram:

> *Get thee out of thy country, and from thy kindred, and from thy father's house, unto a land that I will shew thee: And I will make of thee a great nation, and I will bless thee, and make thy name great, and thou shalt be a blessing. And I will bless them that bless thee, and curse him that curseth thee: and in thee shall all families of the*

earth be blessed. So Abram departed, as the LORD had spoken unto him; and Lot went with him: and Abram was seventy and five years old when he departed out of Haran.

Unlike at the beginning when God spoke to Adam and Eve as one, here we see God only speaking to Abram. When God speaks to Abram and tells him to go, Sarai is not around to receive confirmation. When you are married, you don't have the luxury of making your own decisions, even in something as significant as moving your entire family to another country. God does not speak to Sarai, nor does Abram ask for her opinion. Verse five tells us that Abram took his wife along with his nephew, cattle and other possessions.

A new age wife may be offended by being taken as a piece of property. Media constantly tells women to be seen and heard, speak their minds and don't let anyone run over them, but the Bible teaches us otherwise. We should *be quick to hear and slow to speak and slow to anger* (James 1:19). We should *submit ourselves one to another out of reverence for Christ* (Ephesians 5:21). How many times have we interrupted the plan of God by talking too much? Imagine if Abram had told Sarai they were leaving and she'd immediately began complaining. We just left, we're old, I'll miss my family, and we've never seen a promised land. While these are all valid concerns, Abram had a word from the Lord.

Due to Sarai's position of influence with her husband, she could have changed his mind and talked Abram out of following the word of the Lord. Sometimes, we talk ourselves out of opportunities, talk over a good man and talk while God is trying to speak. Often, we need to be quiet and have faith that God is working out all things for our good. There are many times when husbands go to their wives for advice. I am a huge proponent of making joint decisions, whether large or small. However, I also understand the need for submission and order. Husbands are visionaries and need the freedom to dream. If they are bound to a wife's opinion every time they need to make a decision, this will inhibit them from taking risks and growing in the confidence of who God called them to be. The life of a nomad models how life married to a visionary will be. Like Sarai, every Sidechick needs to have faith to follow.

Even after God promises to bless Abram and his seed, they ran into another crisis. There was a drought. Therefore, Abram, Lot and Sarai needed to go through Egypt. Abram attempt to protect himself and Sarai pretended that his wife was his sister. He reasoned that the Egyptians would kill him to have Sarai if they knew that she was his wife. This was another reason for Sarai to complain. Not only were they going back through Egypt, a place of bondage, but they could have been killed in the process. Being a Sidechick to a great visionary will require you to do things that don't always make sense. In fact, most of what you are required to do will seem ludicrous. It will go against common sense, and you won't be able to find a model for it. Confirmation may or may not come, and your faith will often be tested. You must first have faith in God, and secondly, have faith in your husband. I promise you if you follow a man who is following Christ, God will bless you abundantly.

Sarai, somewhere along the line, got tired of being barren. God spoke to Abram but did not speak to Sarai during this time. In fact, God changed both Abram and Sarai's names to Abraham and Sarah respectively, for they would be the father and mother of many nations. I believe Sarah felt forgotten and alone due to her condition. She took matters into her own hands and arranged for Abraham to have a child with another woman. Because of her influence with her husband, Abraham agreed and slept with Hagar, the handmaiden. As a result, the couple had a son whom they named Ishmael. Abraham loved Ishmael dearly. He even prayed that God would bless him, while God was still saying that Sarah would have a son. Look at the mess Sarah caused by stepping out of line. While she should have been following her husband, she was off making her plan. When you can't see or hear what God is saying to your husband, you need faith to follow.

As you can see, Sarah's faith didn't start when she heard the men tell Abraham she would have a child. Her faith started at the very beginning. She had to follow Abraham when he was still Abram from place to place with no surety of God's plan. She had faith to follow, even through loss, famine and near death experiences. As a Sidechick, your faith to follow will surely be tested. Men gain the strength they need to go forward when people follow their lead. If you are wondering what to do when your husband seems to be taking you down an unfamiliar path, refer back to the chapter on intercession. Remember, your job is to submit and you will surely need faith to do that.

Faith to Look Forward

Before we get to the laugh, I want to discuss how a lack of faith may look. Sometimes, God gives us a promise and tells us to do a thing. We are reluctantly obedient. We complain while we move and don't believe that what God said will happen. Note that this is not the same as moving forward with fear. If you are truly hearing from God, the moves you are required to make will cause you to be afraid. What I am referring to is doing something without faith. Hebrews 11:6 says:

> But without faith, it is impossible to please Him, for he who comes to God must believe that He is and that He is a rewarder of those who diligently seek Him.

In Genesis 19, we see obedience without faith in Lot's wife. God instructs Lot to get out of Gomorrah and go into a small town outside of the city's limits. The Lord had decided to destroy Sodom and Gomorrah because of their wickedness. Abraham moved God to save his nephew, Lot, and his family. In verse 17, God gave Lot some specific instructions:

> And it came to pass when they had brought them forth abroad, that he said, Escape for thy life; look not behind thee, neither stay thou in all the plain; escape to the mountain, lest thou be consumed.

Later, in that same chapter, we see what happened and how Lot's family was saved.

> The sun rose upon the earth when Lot entered into Zoar.
> Then the LORD rained upon Sodom and upon Gomorrah brimstone and fire from the LORD out of heaven;
> And he overthrew those cities, and all the plain, and all the inhabitants of the

cities, and that which grew upon the ground.
But his wife looked back from behind him, and she became a pillar of salt.

Here, we see what happens when you lack faith in the word of the Lord. You may disobey or only partially obey what God tells you to do. It may seem harsh that Lot's wife was turned into a pillar of salt just for looking behind her, but you have to understand what she was looking for. Did she need confirmation that the city was being destroyed? Maybe she looked back and missed what she had back there, or maybe she was just rebellious. They had specific instructions to get out and not look back, or they would be destroyed. Either way, she did not have what she needed to survive what was coming. She needed to be fully persuaded by God's promises. She had to leave what was behind her to move forward. Her lack of faith caused her to miss out on the perfect plan of God. To be a Sidechick, you must have faith to go forward.

Faith to Laugh

Finally, let's discuss the laughter. The Hebrew word for a laugh is *tsâchaq,* meaning to laugh outright, mock, play or do sport. Now that we have a better understanding of Abraham and Sarah's journey, we should agree that when Abraham and Sarah laughed, it wasn't because they lacked faith. Abraham and Sarah had a lifetime of proof that they indeed had faith. Abraham was 75 years old when God spoke to him and made the covenant to give them a son. It wasn't until 24 years later at the ages of 99 and 89 respectively that the angels of the Lord visited Abraham and Sarah. They confirmed and reminded Abraham of what God had already spoken. However, this time Sarah was within earshot.

Like Adam needed Eve, Abraham needed Sarah's faith to obtain this promise. There are times when God just requires you to go along and follow your husband. There are other times when you must come into agreement with what God is trying to do.

Sarah laughed because it was impossible for a woman of her age to have children. She was physically past child-bearing age. She and Abraham lacked the faculties to conceive a child. After everything they had been through, God was still manifesting His covenant with them. I'm sure I would have laughed too.

In Genesis 21, at Abraham's tender age of 100, Isaac was born. Sarah sums up the purpose of her laughter in verse 6 saying:

> *God hath made me laugh so that all that hear will laugh with me.*

The Hebrew word used for hearing is *shâma* which means to hear intelligently. So anyone who hears her story will understand the impossibility of the situation and the power of God will be made known. The laughter of Abraham and Sarah was not an indication of the size of their faith. Instead, it was an indication of the magnitude of their situation. Sarah's faith was so great that she was mentioned in what some would call faith's hall of fame. Hebrews 11:11 is a record of Sarah's faith. It reads:

> *By faith, Sarah herself also received strength to conceive seed, and she bore a child[ ] when she was past the age because she judged Him faithful who had promised.*

Whatever God has spoken to you and your husband, let Abraham and Sarah's story inspire you. Remember to keep your faith regardless of how ridiculous the situation seems. Know that God is ready to keep His promise and your faith will cause you to see it.

CHAPTER 8

Survivor

The date is January 21, 1998. It is eight o'clock in the morning, and the house is already buzzing with activity. The phone rings, the vacuum roars and the television blasts the news. The constant lull is almost impossible to bear. Finally, I succumb to the pressure and answer the call on the fourth and final ring.

> "Hello," I manage to mutter.
> "Hey! I'm so sorry about the news. There was nothing we could do to stop it; we had no idea," a familiar voice says from across the line.
> "What news? I was barely out of bed. What's going on?"
> "Oh dear. I hate to be the one to break it to you. Do me a favor and check the Washington Post. Front page, dead center," she says. "And try not to worry; everything will be okay."

*"Okay," I say, still confused. "I'll call you
back," I mumble, thinking what could
be so urgent to call me so early.*

*I reach over to find my glasses and slip them
on just over my nose for comfort. I turn over,
but the bed is empty. My husband had an early
day again, I think to myself. I slip out of bed,
feeling kind of confused, but desperate to have
some answers. What is it that's so pressing,
but not urgent enough that Bill would call? As
normal, outside my door, the newspaper
bundle awaits.*

SCANDAL in the WHITE HOUSE, *the title
reads, and a knot forms in my stomach.*
***"President Has Affair with White House
Aide,"*** *the caption further explains. Initial
shock followed by disbelief soon turns to
anger and rage. How could he? Why would
he? What did I do to deserve this? So many
questions, but never the right answers. I just
need to get away. Oh, my goodness ... my
daughter, my family, my life ... I just can't deal
with this all today. I'd always had a hunch, but*

never in a million years would I have believed that this could be true. I take off my glasses as the tears cover my lenses, making it impossible to see. I lie back down and bury my head, thinking this has got to be a bad dream. Unable to sleep, I realize that I must confront this head on. I call my husband and right away, he stammers, "It's not true. You have to believe me."

Furious, ashamed, hateful, alone and overwhelmed are just a few of the emotions I felt over the next few months as the situation unfolded. Although my husband finally admitted that the allegations were true, my stance has never changed. I am committed to standing by my husband through the guilt and shame and seeing our family win.
~fictional account based on the true story of Clinton White House scandal in 1998.

This chapter is particularly difficult to write and may be the most difficult for any woman to swallow. It is important to understand that the basis of this chapter is a revelation from the word of God, not the world's book of hard knocks. Often, some situations arise in a marriage that could lead to divorce. Let me make the clear distinction that I am specifically addressing areas that arise *after* marriage, not before. *Identifying red flags before marriage is a different topic for another book, but let me address a few things while we're here.* There is a fight that you have for your marriage that you aren't obligated to engage in outside of the covenant. The dating and engagement phase of a relationship are important for trying a person's character and establishing a strong foundation of love, trust and respect. Often, in a rush to get married, we ignore the signs of a failed relationship. Aggressiveness, insecurity, depression and unfaithfulness should be addressed in premarital counseling or used as a filtering system for determining your level of readiness for marriage. If you see signs of things that may negatively impact you or your marriage, address them!

Infidelity, mismanagement of resources
and forms of dishonor are just a few
categories of issues that may arise in
marriage. As a *Sidechick*, you must fight for
your marriage, regardless of the cost. In
addition to pride and emotional hurt, family
and friends may encourage you during these
times to just "take care of you." The pressure
of being looked at as weak, desperate or just
plain dumb may allow you to think that
leaving is the best or only answer. I
admonish you, however, to diligently seek
the Lord concerning what you should do. You
may be surprised, and your views may be
challenged by the instructions you receive.

Forgive

When someone hurts you, it is human
nature to defend yourself or retaliate.
However, in a marriage, one must constantly
forgive. This is not a sign of weakness, but
rather a sign of strength and faith. It takes a
great deal of humility to forgive others who
have wronged you. In Matthew 18:21-22,
Jesus discusses the topic of forgiveness.

Then came Peter to him, and said, Lord, how oft shall my brother sin against me, and I forgive him? Till seven times?Jesus saith unto him, I say not unto thee, Until seven times: but, Until seventy times seven.

In Matthew 6, the Lord's Prayer says to forgive others their trespasses as God has forgiven you. Like the love that Christ has for His bride, the church, so too must we demonstrate this unfailing love for our spouses. The word of God says that *"love covers a multitude of sins."* Additionally, the word says, *"No greater love than this, than for a man to lay down his life for a friend."* Jesus took away all the guilt and shame and the death associated with sin when He laid down His life on the cross. He knew no sin, but became our sins that we would live for eternity. How much more then should we seek to forgive and restore our spouses when they do us wrong?

Let's take a look at the life of Hosea and Gomer for a lesson in effectual love, forgiveness and restoration.

In Hosea 1, we witness God instructing Hosea to take a prostitute for a wife. This effectual love story would be a shadow of the love of God for His people. One would assume that the woman immediately turned away from her life as a prostitute once Hosea took her as his wife. I mean, if someone is willing to love you and take you in after knowing how many men you've slept with and manipulated, you would think she would have been overwhelmed by his love. But she had no desire to make the marriage work. In fact, God had to speak to Hosea again and tell him to go out and find his wandering wife who'd returned to her previous lifestyle.

"Heartbroken, Hosea raised the children and desperately missed his wife. After a period God returned to Hosea with the message to go out in search of Gomer and to bring her home. Hosea found his wife in all her debauchery

127

and brought her back where he continued to love her and tend to her needs. God uses this peculiar story to illustrate the unfailing love he has for his people." ~ From Women of Faith blog

This just doesn't make sense. Why would God allow Hosea and the children to experience so much pain? You must understand that the story is much bigger than them. God was demonstrating His love for His people, who'd disobeyed His word time after time. Hosea mirrors the constancy of God's love. *In Hosea 14:4, He says, "I will heal their backsliding. I will love them freely."* Did Gomer deserve that kind of forgiveness? Do we? God's love extends beyond the limits of our sinful humanity. No matter where we go or what we have done, God's love and grace cover us.

This story, although a shadow or type of God's love for His people, has natural implications in marriage. Our love for our spouses should survive the scandal. If your

SURVIVOR

spouse has a gambling habit and constantly spends the money you save, should you leave or are you the key to unlocking deliverance, healing and restoration in your spouse? Will your prayers and faith in God be what turns the heart of your spouse? If your spouse has cheated on you, is it your immediate response to leave or do you begin to pray? Pray for your spouse's healing, pray for your marriage and ask God for the courage to stay and fight. Notice that God was constantly leading Hosea. He didn't stay in the marriage and just let things go haywire. He also wasn't constantly arguing, bitter or blaming God. He was purposeful in his pursuit and serving of his wife's needs. She needed some specific, intentional care to come out of prostitution.

If we are honest, we all have something that we need specific treatment to recover from, whether it is the loss of a parent at a young age, an abusive relationship or molestation. All of these have an impact on our character and relationships with other people. As a wife, we must be knowledgeable of these factors and spiritually minded to attack them. The man should also be aware of your issues and be willing to go with you through the process of being healed. According to the Bible, *we wrestle not against flesh and blood but against every principality that exalts itself against the authority of God.* We must understand that our spouses are not the enemy; the other woman is not the enemy. Our roles are much more than about us being happy and having everything that we want. Our spouses, our children, our communities and the generations to come are counting on us to build and sustain healthy marriages.

There are plenty of other examples of marriages between famous people that were destroyed by divorce. The life and legacy of some are so badly overshadowed by the stench of divorce that they never fully recover. For others, the rumors of infidelity or other marital problems remain hearsay and are never fully exposed. Finally, there are those who stay married after a scandal has been proven and verified. When both parties repent, turn away from their sins and seek the Lord for guidance, it is possible to recover from a marital scandal. It takes consistent prayer, meaningful time of restoration and continually seeking the Lord for help. When we look at the example of the Clintons, they have survived several years since the scandal broke and have even made history! The wife became the first woman to ever receive a nomination from a major political party for President of the United States. What an honor and a true testament to what you should do when scandal hits. SURVIVE!

CHAPTER 9

Redeemed

For three nights in a row, her husband had gone out with his friends. It was NBA All-Star weekend, and all of the celebrities were in town. There were events all over the city, and he had tickets to what seemed like all of them. With two young children at home, she didn't have much time or energy to go out anymore, but somehow, her husband made it work. He didn't help with anything around the house and didn't make her job as a mom any easier. This is not how she imagined her marriage would be. He had always been loving, respectful and a provider for their family, but after the second kid came along, things began to change. She suffered from postpartum depression and was no longer her carefree self. But he didn't provide her with any relief. He wasn't sympathetic and just didn't seem to care. Every time she tried to talk to him about *what was going on, he blew it off like she was over dramatic. Months passed and they grew further apart. She slowly came out of her depression, and they continued to grow apart.*

But this All-star weekend took her over the edge. Her friends began to ask her why her husband was hardly around. She was embarrassed to say that her husband was out with his friends or away on a guys' trip, while she stayed at home with the kids, so she decided to talk to her girlfriend, a woman in her life group, about what was going on. Her girlfriend encouraged her to bring him to the marriage retreat with a few other couples. She raved about how this event changed her marriage for the better the previous year.

After weeks of resistance, she was finally able to convince her husband to go to the retreat. They had a husbands-only session, where men shared some of their struggles in marriage. While in that session, her husband had a complete revelation of how his actions had negatively impacted his wife and their family.

He was embarrassed and wanted to make up for everything he had done. When they got home, he prepared a wonderful, private evening away from the kids. He bought her gifts and spent the whole night making her feel like a queen. At the end of the night, he apologized for everything he had done. To his surprise, she did not accept his apology. Instead, she wanted to know why he'd taken her through so much pain. He was unable to give a good explanation other than that he was young and immature. She told him she was tired of his excuses, didn't believe a word he said and would be moving out the next day. They were separated for a year before officially divorcing. The wife just could not get over the past.

Rahab was a harlot. For most people, her name stops there, but when I read her story, I see much more. A woman of detestable beginnings, she'd reduced her femininity to her sexuality, and her reputation around the city preceded her. Everyone knew Rahab and the life she lived, but when the Israelite men came to spy on Jericho, her life changed forever.

I believe many marriages have tough beginnings. You are combining two individuals with different families, a variety of experiences and possibly different fundamental beliefs. Coming together to be one flesh will not be easy. You will disagree, misunderstand each other and possibly even disrespect one another. You will be new in your role as wife and will certainly make mistakes, but let Rahab's story of redemption encourage you to keep going.

Early on in my marriage, my husband and I got into a huge argument while visiting one of our friends. My husband had asked me to do something, but I refused. Looking back, I have no idea why I was so stubborn. When we left, we had a huge blowout about how disrespectful I was. My intent at the time was not to be disrespectful. I felt like the request was not that important, and I just didn't feel like doing it. Of course, the issue was not the request. The problem was that I belittled him by not doing what he'd asked me to do, not to mention the fact that we were in front of other people. I must have looked like a monster and a terrible wife, but thank God, I learned and have never done that again. Many marriages never recover from something like that. Sometimes, the offended party never lets it go. Other times, the offender never admits their wrong-doing. The key to longevity in marriage is not perfection. The key is being quick to forgive and committed to restoration. Let's take a look at Rahab on her road to redemption.

We meet Rahab in Joshua 2 when Joshua sends spies to scope out the city of Jericho. God told Joshua that He would give him and the Israelites this land. Rahab risked her life when she lied to the king's men, telling them that the Israelites had already left. After this, she shared with the Israelites what she knew.

Before the spies lay down for the night, she went up on the roof [9] and said to them, "I know that the LORD has given you this land and that a great fear of you has fallen on us, so that all who live in this country are melting in fear because of you. We had heard how the LORD dried up the water of the Red Sea for you when you came out of Egypt, and what you did to Sihon and Og, the two kings of the Amorites east of the Jordan, whom you destroyed. When we heard of it, our hearts melted in fear and everyone's courage failed because of you, for the LORD your God is God in heaven above and on the earth below. (Joshua 2: 8-11)

I am sure most of the information she'd gathered had come from all of the men who passed through her house, but what she shared was also a revelation. Not only did she know what had happened, but she also understood why it'd happened. She said, "For the Lord, your God is God in heaven above and on the earth below." The beginning of redemption begins with knowledge and grows with revelation.

Going back to the incident described earlier, we had to be clear about what happened. My husband and I don't argue, but we do disagree. The difference is that generally when you argue, you are just trying to get your point across. When you disagree, you need to listen to the other person's point of view. We made an intentional decision to understand why we failed so that we could grow and move on. When you hit trouble in your marriage, be intentional about the outcome you desire. Is this disagreement unto divorce or will your marriage recover?

Rahab continued her exchange with the spies by giving them valuable information about how the people felt about them. She knew that they would soon destroy the city. She then made them promise to save her and her family. Once they agreed, she gave the Israelite spies instructions to make it out of the city.

I believe that when Rahab acknowledged who God was that her life hit a significant turning point. Albeit, the former half of her life was less than admirable, the latter half of her life would be blessed. If your marriage starts off shaky, don't let that be the defining tone. Get an understanding of exactly what is going wrong and commit to recovering. After you have recommitted to your marriage, pray for revelation. In the beginning, it is likely that you won't fully understand how God intends to use your marriage. The more you get revelation, the more committed you will be to forgiving.

When you first get married, you will likely have selfish motives. Some are looking for love, some want to start a family, and others may just want to have sex. At the beginning of our marriages, we are naïve and often have unrealistic expectations. We want our mates to be perfect, even though we are far from it. However, the more we grow in revelation, the more we understand that the purpose of marriage is much greater than ourselves. Your children depend on you, your city needs you, and the world is waiting for you to get it right. It is with this revelation that we learn to forgive and restore one another.

The story of Rahab's escape is told in Joshua 6.

> Joshua said to the two men who had spied out the land, "Go into the prostitute's house and bring her out and all who belong to her, by your oath to her." So the young men who had done the spying went in and brought out Rahab, her father and mother, her brothers and sisters and all who belonged to her. They brought out her entire family and put them in place outside the camp of Israel.

Rahab's refusal to succumb to her past and her belief that God could use a whore like her saved her entire family. But the miracle doesn't stop there. The story goes on to tell us that Rahab married one of the spies and they had a son named Boaz. This is the man who eventually married Ruth and begot Obed, who begot Jesse, father of David, of whose lineage Jesus was born. What a miraculous finish for a harlot! When people look at your marriage, they may say what a miraculous finish for a drug dealer! Or what an extraordinary finish for an adulterer! Or what a miraculous finish for a (you fill in the blank)! What do you want people to look at your marriage and say?

It is very easy to have a traumatic experience and become bitter. You may be angry at God for allowing something so difficult to happen, or you may be angry at your spouse for treating you poorly. But I promise you there is a great reward if can let it go and allow your husband and your marriage to be redeemed.

CHAPTER 10

Sidechicks Hall of Fame

The stories here represent wives with characteristics not previously mentioned in this book. These women have embodied incredible abilities, including boldness, sacrifice, and wisdom. May you find yourself and find encouragement in their stories.

Sidechick #1
Name: Winnie Mandela
Quality: Bold

Her Story:

      Her husband stood for world peace in the midst of war. He believed every man was created equal and deserved to be treated equally. In a country where he was considered a second-class citizen, he stood up for what he believed. He broke laws he believed were unfair and went to jail for crimes he did not commit. The unjust police force considered him a rebel. The corrupt government considered him a threat to the organized slavery and system of brutality. He spoke up when told to be quiet. He was a voice for the voiceless. He organized riots against the government and mobilized an entire nation of people. They called him a hero, but they slandered his wife for doing the same. If you are a citizen of the great country of South Africa, Winnie Mandela continues to be a great source of controversy. Was she guilty of crimes against her people, or was she unfairly judged for exhibiting the ruthlessness reserved for men in her time? I will let you be the judge.

For you:

If you are a Sidechick married to a visionary, you may find yourself in Winnie's shoes. You have to protect your family, you have given up everything for the cause, and then, the people betray you. Your husband is heralded as a hero, but you find yourself put to shame. People may say you are too aggressive. They fail to see that you are also on the front lines fighting for the vision.

Proverbs 28:1 tells us *"The wicked flee when no man pursueth: but the righteous are bold as a lion."*

Your fight won't always be pretty. You will have to speak for the voiceless or stand up against injustice. You will have to beat systems designed to keep you bound. If God has called you to speak up, don't let people intimidate you and cause you to keep quiet. You need the wisdom of God to navigate the terrain and still maintain the character of Jesus Christ.

Sidechick #2
Name: Hannah
Quality: Sacrifice

Her Story:
She was one of two wives of a wealthy man named Elkanah. His other wife was fruitful and had given him many children, but

Hannah was barren. Every year when Elkanah would go up to worship, he would give the wives portions. He loved Hannah and would always give her a double portion, but Hannah desired to have a child and would not be settled until she did. The other wife would provoke Hannah, which caused her to retreat and withdraw. Hannah did not eat and was deeply saddened by her dilemma. She prayed incessantly and refused to give up hope. One day, she promised God that if she had a child, she would give the child back to Him. The great priest, Eli, showed up to bring confirmation from God. He'd heard her prayers, seen her sacrifice and would indeed bless her with a child. When her son, Samuel, was born, she did just what she'd promised. She nursed him until he was old enough to go on his own. After this, she left him in the hands of the priest, Eli, in the temple to serve God all the days of his life.

For you:

Sidechicks sacrifice. You may work hard and long days, only to build your husband's dream. You may give up fancy vacations and a life you've always imagined to see God's plan revealed in your husband. Although Hannah sacrificed her long-awaited blessing, God blessed her with even more than she could imagine. Hannah went on to have more children and was able to see Samuel grow up serving the Lord. Samuel became one of the greatest prophets of all time. Although Hannah had to make a great sacrifice, in the end, she received a much greater reward. You may be giving up your plans, money, time or a dream, but just remember that the word of God tells us:

> *Give, and it shall be given unto you;*
> *good measure, pressed*
> *down, and shaken*
> *together, and running*
> *over, shall men give into your bosom.*
> *For with the same measure that ye*

*mete withal, it shall be measured to you
again.*
(Luke 6:38 KJV)

Hannah's story of sacrifice and reward
can be found in 1 Samuel.

Sidechick #3
Name: Coretta Scott King
Quality: Courageous

Her Story:

Coretta Scott King was the wife of
Reverend Dr. Martin Luther King Jr.,
heralded as one of the most important voices
of the Civil Rights Movement. Dr. King is
known for disrupting the "normal" attitude
and behavior of the majority in American
society. He challenged segregation,
institutional racism and other unfair
treatment of African Americans. He led
peaceful protests, boycotts and organized
resistance. You can imagine that this came at
a cost. Mrs. King received death threats

constantly, and their home was even bombed. With four children, a congregation and a world of followers, they had a lot to lose.

For you:

When you are married to someone who challenges the standard, be prepared for the backlash. Everyone will not like or support you. Stand beside your husband and give him the motivation to keep going. I can imagine Dr. King being on the road, fearing for his life and thinking of his family back at home. He'd been in and out of jail, beaten and spit on. Mrs. King had to have the courage not to give up. For every person who publicly cheers you on, there are those behind the scenes waiting for your downfall. After Dr. King's untimely assassination, Mrs. King continued to build the legacy they'd started together. In Joshua 1:9, the Lord encourages Joshua after Moses dies.

> *Have not I commanded thee? Be strong and of good courage; be not afraid,*

neither be thou dismayed: for the LORD thy God is with thee whithersoever thou goest.

I pray that God gives you the courage to stand up against those who don't want change ... to stand with your husband and build the vision that you were born to fulfill.

Sidechick #4
Name: Michelle Obama
Quality: Pioneer

Her Story:

In 2008, she became the first African American first lady married to the first African American president of the United States. In a country with a government over two hundred years old, the election was nothing short of astonishing. With no model to follow, she had the arduous task of blazing the pathway. Like the first, she couldn't compare herself to anyone else, which is both a relief and an enormous responsibility.

Expectations were high, and the pressure was immense from both critics and supporters alike. What should she wear? What should she say? How should she speak? Critics complained when her attire was too expensive and even labeled her an angry black woman for her opinionated views. It was almost as if she couldn't win, but she took on the challenge with grace. She and her husband won a second term in office and left a legacy that will never be forgotten. Breaking traditions and engaging audiences in politics who had never been involved before.

For you:

Sidechicks often have to go first. A man with a vision will seem crazy for doing things that have never been done. A pioneer faces challenges that have never been seen and will, therefore, have to conquer them without an example of what to do. Those who go first must be selfless. If it weren't for those who are coming behind, they might give up in the process. If you are first, remember that your labor is not in vain. Women and families are coming behind you who need you to win. Your commitment to the vision is making way for those who will come after you. You are shaking up the monotony of what was and preparing the world for what is to come. When you feel like you're alone and are unsure of how to proceed, seek the word of the Lord. Psalms 199:105 reminds us: *Thy word is a lamp unto my feet and a light unto my path.*

I pray that God gives you direction as you go first. And may you have comfort knowing that He will never leave or forsake you.

Sidechick # 5
Name: You
Qualities: All of the above

Your story:

What is your story? What is your claim to fame? Do your husband and children rise and call you blessed?

All of us come from different backgrounds. We have different experiences, both good and bad, that shape the way we view life. Examples in our lives also shape how we interpret marriage. Check your history and understand how that impacts your relationships and view of yourself. Understand that you have a significant role to play in fulfilling the vision of God for your family. God created man and woman and blessed THEM. Go forward with assurance that the world needs you to fulfill the vision. You are a Sidechick, married to the visionary and called for such a time as this!

Made in the USA
Middletown, DE
07 April 2018